The Art of SERIES
EDITED BY CHARLES BAXTER

The Art of series is a line of books reinvigorating the practice of craft and criticism. Each book is a brief, witty, and useful exploration of fiction, nonfiction, or poetry by a writer impassioned by a singular craft issue. *The Art of* volumes provide a series of sustained examinations of key, but sometimes neglected, aspects of creative writing by some of contemporary literature's finest practitioners.

THE ART OF INTIMACY

THE SPACE BETWEEN

The Art of

INTIMACY

THE SPACE BETWEEN

Stacey D'Erasmo

Graywolf Press

This publication is made possible, in part, by the voters of Minnesota through a Minnesota State Arts Board Operating Support grant, thanks to a legislative appropriation from the arts and cultural heritage fund, and through a grant from the National Endowment for the Arts. Significant support has also been provided by Target, the McKnight Foundation, Amazon.com, and other generous contributions from foundations, corporations, and individuals. To these organizations and individuals we offer our heartfelt thanks.

Published by Graywolf Press
212 Third Avenue North, Suite 485
Minneapolis, Minnesota 55401

www.graywolfpress.org

Published in the United States of America

ISBN 978-1-55597-647-7

4 6 8 10 9 7 5 3

Library of Congress Control Number: 2013931486

Cover design: Scott Sorenson

Contents

The kindly way to feel separating is to have a space between. This shows a likeness.

—Gertrude Stein, "Roast Beef," from *Tender Buttons*

THE ART OF INTIMACY

THE SPACE BETWEEN

Trying to See

What is the nature of intimacy, of what happens in the space between us? And how do we, as writers, catch or reflect it on the page? One hesitates, perhaps, to be so direct. Like looking directly at the sun, looking directly at the creation of intimacy in fiction seems like a dangerous business. In art as in life, one wishes intimacy to be, or at least to seem, unspoken, unmanipulated, certainly unforced. And, of course, when I talk about intimacy, I'm not only talking about romantic relationships between consenting adults. Friendships, the bonds of parents and children, the fleeting communion of strangers at a dinner party or on a train or a plane, crushes, being deeply moved by art or by a historical event, the relationship between reader and writer: in all of these, that space between is vital, electric, and it often drives the story. *Only connect,* wrote Forster, and we do, for better and for worse; we exhort our characters to do the same.

Moreover, we insist that, in literature, these connections must earn their keep by carrying meaning. They must speak some sort of truth about human existence— ethereal, carnal, primal, fleeting, damaging, reparative, beautiful, terrifying, exalted, base, ambiguous, or any combination thereof, these meetings of minds, hearts, and bodies take on a special gravity on the page. We measure their weight against our own experience. As with all other matters in fiction, the composition of these intimacies appears to us to pick out a pattern in the plenitude of everyday life, to find the chord in the cacophony of the street. *And then they lived happily ever after.* This is not the part of the story that engages us. We want to know what they said, how they looked, what was exchanged between them, what it all meant, and how it went down. Who was lost, who was found, and why? Every time one character approaches another, makes that perilous crossing into the space between, the reader knows that what happens next will be critical, it will produce a change. When we read a well-wrought piece of fiction, we long for that change, for the good or the ill, to occur.

Recently, I was waiting for a visitor to arrive. His plane was delayed. To pass the time and because I wanted to see it, I went to the Matthew Marks Gallery to see the Nan Goldin photo exhibit *Scopophilia.* In this project, Goldin was invited by the Louvre to pair photos of hers with imagery from the painting and sculpture in the museum. Goldin was given access to the Louvre in the off-hours so that she could take photos of the artwork that interested her. She paired four hundred images of hers with images from pieces in the Louvre; in addition to these framed pairings, she created a twenty-five-minute-long slide installation. The slide installation combines images of her work and of work in the Louvre with classical music composed by Alain Mahé and a musing voiceover composed of Goldin's thoughts on the work and readings from Ovid's *Metamorphoses,* St. Teresa, and others.

Goldin's work, which first came to prominence with her 1986 series of photos *The Ballad of Sexual Dependency,* is intensely personal. Throughout her career, she has focused on taking photographs of friends and lovers of both genders at their most naked, often literally. Here is her ex-lover Siobhan getting out of the shower, arms upraised, the look on her face both seductive and challenging. Here is a young man with extraordinary ice-blue eyes, naked, smoking, the look on his face both seductive and challenging. Here are families with children, women alone, drag queens and transsexuals, naked pregnant women, couples sleeping, children playing, people making love, men and women looking directly into the camera with frank desire or aggravation or hostility or affection, or all of these at once, and often with a clear pleasure in being looked at. As the art critic Vince Aletti has written, she has been the "prime iconographer of the downtown scene, a pansexual bohemia on the verge of a nervous breakdown." Goldin, as a vulnerable member of that bohemia, has been her own subject many times—she has photographed herself with her eyes blackened by a lover, naked in bed staring at a (presumably unringing) phone, in moments of joy, of pain, of confusion, of connection and disconnection.

Her great subject has been intimacy in all forms, among all genders, and in all emotional modes. In the Louvre—one of the less intimate spaces on the planet—Goldin found a treasure house of intimate moments, gestures, gazes, facial expressions, and bodily positions. She focused in on details from larger, grander works to discover the crook of a lover's arm around another, a face carved from marble turned at the most tender of angles, skeins of hair flowing over an exposed breast, mutual gazes, and many physical curves and hollows. We notice anew the curve of Cleopatra's breasts in *Cleopatra with the Asp;* the lyricism of a naked back in *Cupid with His Wings on Fire;* the downward tilt of Galatea's chin in *Pygmalion and Galatea.* These details, paired with her modern subjects in ordinary rooms and landscapes, might suggest an aggrandizement of the present moment—here's how my hot girlfriend looks just like *Winged Victory* getting out of the shower—but actually the pairings work the other way around, by reminding us that these august paintings and sculptures are impressions, painstakingly rendered, of living human beings, now gone. These works of art are also vivid fossils of intimacy. To Goldin, the human connection, and the yearning for that connection, are everywhere, even in the most exalted and reified spaces. Moreover, she never gets tired of looking at them. *Scopophilia*, after all, means the love of looking, or, as Goldin puts it, "the intense desire—and the fulfillment of that desire—experienced through looking." One of the desires prominently on display in this exhibition was Goldin's unabashed desire to look, and look again, and look still more. Walking into the Louvre at night for the first time, Goldin says in the voiceover, she was surprised by her own "very intense reaction" to the visual abundance that surrounded her.

As I sat in the dark watching the slide show, I can't say that I experienced such intense visual ecstasy, but my own loneliness and impatience for my visitor to arrive started to melt away. However, this was certainly not the grandeur of the Louvre after hours. The small viewing gallery was about half-full; in front of me, two elderly women, one in a wheelchair, bickered loudly over the strains of the slow, rich sound track. But the images were engaging and beautiful, transporting. Each one suggested a story half-glimpsed: what happened with that dark-eyed woman after the shutter clicked? What is the question silently being asked by that lithe, dangerous-seeming man, and why? Who is the tall, middle-aged woman, naked, on a rock, and who is she to Goldin? Who are the men floating in water? Goldin reveals the people again and again, and by implication her great desire to look at them. But we, the viewers, do not know their stories nor what place any of them occupies in Goldin's life. We only know that none of them is a stranger to her. But while the exact details of these subjects' lives remain private, Goldin's relationship to our voyeurism is never coy. *Yeah,* she seems to say, *that's how it is for me, too.* The very beauty of the images, a generous and persistent beauty of light and composition, feels like love, even, at times, like limerence. Goldin invites us to see the men and women she loves as she sees them, to occupy her position as loving eye. She gazes with equal intensity at the human subjects and the details from the art, as if, within her gaze, the distinction between the animate and the inanimate is rather slight. We feel, perhaps, closer to, or attracted to, these subjects, but we probably feel closest psychically to Goldin; we understand what her desire feels like to her.

Yeah, I thought that afternoon, *that's how it is for me, too.* And so I felt, for those moments in the dark, seen and accompanied. I did not, though, feel accompanied by or especially identified with Goldin's images themselves, as beautiful as they were, and as familiar as the modern, generally urban subjects are to me. I did not feel accompanied by the details from Delacroix or Bronzino, exquisite though they were. I felt accompanied by the fragile, transitory triangle of photographer, image, and viewer, a momentary space between self and others mediated by the artist's composition, doubled by the artist's composition of earlier artists' compositions in a kind of hall of mirrors of gazes. I was compelled, as well, by the electricity of the juxtapositions. The juxtaposition, for instance, of an image of the actress Tilda Swinton staring, flanked by leopards, with an image of a marble woman on a marble horse set off a series of reverberations and associations about femininity, wildness, and an odd sort of fixity, about marblelike flesh and fleshlike marble.

And what of the artist who had placed one image next to the other, what did the space between them reveal? "Between them and me," says Goldin on the voiceover, "telepathic exchanges, divination." Part of the pleasure of the slide show and exhibit lay in that unnameable zone of "telepathic exchanges" where the artist had chosen to put one image beside the other—in the connection she saw, for instance, between images from '80s club life and various veiled figures carved from marble. Goldin shows the viewer people who may or may not look like intimates of one's own, but she also locates the viewer exactly in that space between self and other, and in the longing to be in that space. We remember our own various desires to look. We see and we feel that we are not alone there.

The artist's illusion had worked for me that afternoon. While I was waiting for my visitor, something else had arrived in the dark, something furred and feathered and bejeweled, prismatic, playful, ambiguous, and, quietly, melancholy. (One cannot quite shake the feeling that the continual creation and evocation of connection must have some relationship to its opposite, which is rather conspicuous by its absence.) Goldin's slide show created out of high art a zone in which the curatorial principle, across centuries, was the intensity of the intimate moment. The darkness, the music, the play of light and form and color, what I saw and what I couldn't see, the motion of my own guesses and fantasies about the people in the photographs, the demiarticulated narrative and dream space of the slide show, had produced in me a sense of being included, of being intimate, here in the irreal world of art. It wasn't because I was in any of those modern rooms with any of those modern people, nor was I in the Louvre after hours. It was because I was sitting in the dark with strangers on an ordinary weekday in Chelsea, suspended in the space between self and image. When my visitor arrived at last, I wanted to explain all this to him, it seemed important, but I wasn't quite sure how to do it.

Consider what follows part of that explanation. Because I write fiction, I am often trying to develop various sorts of intimacies on the page. My tools are different from Goldin's: language, dialogue, scene, characters who have to eat and drink and walk around in a world of time instead of the color and light and shapes of visual composition. I often fail. I have come to wonder, What's in that critical space between in fiction? Of what is it composed? What makes it "work" or not? One way into this delicate matter might be to look not so much at individual characters and their motivations or the outcomes of their yearnings and relationships, or even at their interactions per se, but at exactly what is in that space between them, the linkage. Another way to put this might be to say: Where do they meet? How does the text bring them together? What electricity do we feel from the juxtaposition? I have noticed that the intimacy we feel as readers is often generated far less by characters turning to one another and saying intimate things or doing intimate things than it is by a kind of textual atmosphere, or maybe one should say a biosphere, a gallery, a zone that both emanates from the characters and acts upon them very deeply and personally. In other words, the textual *where* of their

meetings, the meeting ground, the figurative topos—
and by this I don't mean physical locations where characters meet, but locutions, places in language that they
share—actually produces not only opportunities for intimacy, but also the actual sense of intimacy. That odd
and powerful space between, the space where we meet,
isn't only the medium for intimacy: it is, sometimes,
the thing itself.

This book will not tell you how to write intimate
scenes, nor instruct you on what is a "successful" rendering of intimacy and what is not. There are as many ways
of rendering intimacy as there are of being intimate; an
encyclopedic approach would be a Casaubonesque en-
deavor. Instead, we will venture together into a few of
the meeting places, the spaces between, that have oc-
curred in fiction. We will consider what has happened
there.

Meeting in the *If*

In the idiosyncratic and inventive 1999 movie *Being John Malkovich,* directed by Spike Jonze, the characters played by Catherine Keener and Cameron Diaz, via a means that was never precisely explained, would jointly sort of inhabit the body and mind of John Malkovich—Malkovich played himself in the movie—in which interesting vehicle they were conducting an affair. One of the most hilarious, and perhaps disturbing, recurrent lines in the movie was "Meet you in Malkovich," which was what the lovers said to one another when they wanted to meet. It's impossible to know exactly what screenwriter Charlie Kaufman may have had in mind when he constructed this scenario, but, among other things, it certainly foregrounded a quality peculiar to the actor John Malkovich, which is the quality of never seeming to be entirely real or to fully inhabit his own skin. It seems, on an intuitive if not a realistic level, that one could, actually, meet in Malkovich, because it's never clear if he is, in fact, entirely John Malkovich or if he's a supposition, an ironic stance, a self-aware pose, John Malkovich playing John Malkovich. There seems to be room in Malkovich for other people, because his own attachment to himself seems so tenuous.

He seems to always be a bit "as if," a bit hypothetical, contingent, which is to say: a subjunctive. What Keener and Diaz were saying to one another was: *Meet me in the subjunctive,* in a possibility. *Meet me in the if.* In the end, their relationship does actually work out, the subjunctive being, perhaps, as good a place to foster intimacy as any other. While it is lovely in real life to meet in real life, on a textual level, as much, if not more, can often be accomplished in the subjunctive, language being uniquely suited to holding open the simultaneous possibility that an event is occurring and not occurring, that this or that might happen if it were to occur. *If I saw you. If we met. If I had gone through that door. If I had found you. If you were here.* The *if* is a wonderful device, because it simultaneously alerts the reader that what is to follow did not happen and allows the reader to engage in the narrative as if it were happening. As a grammar, it's an optical illusion that is also potentially quite a powerful tool for summoning up desire and loss simultaneously and causing the reader to experience both states with equal force.

The writers Elizabeth Bowen and William Maxwell made extraordinary use of the subjunctive in the novels *The House in Paris,* by Bowen, and *So Long, See You Tomorrow,* by Maxwell. Though the exterior narrative frame of these novels has to do with the impact of the relationships between adult lovers, and illicit lovers at that, the deeper, much more distressing, and much more perplexing and tender narratives at the core have to do with a much less nameable and far more delicate intimacy: both novels concern children who meet, quite briefly and by chance, in the "real life" of the novel, but who continue to meet for a much longer time than that in that subjunctive, that "as if," which, as it turns out, is the book, the novel that results from their meeting. The time of these children being physically present with one another is very short, but in both novels it leads to a psychic intimacy that is profound and long-lasting.

In *So Long, See You Tomorrow,* the literal action concerns a murder on a farm in Illinois in the 1920s. One man, Lloyd Wilson, has been sleeping with Fern Smith, wife of Clarence Smith. Lloyd is also married, to Marie. The affair is discovered; Fern takes the kids, leaves Clarence, and ultimately divorces him; Marie will not give Lloyd a divorce. Clarence becomes increasingly despondent and ruined and one day he kills Lloyd, shooting him as he milks a cow. A short time later, Clarence kills himself as well. The lives of all those who are left are shattered. One of Clarence and Fern's children is Cletus Smith, who is thirteen at the time of the murder. The unnamed narrator of the book is a boy of about Cletus's age who lives in the same town with his father and stepmother; his biological mother died of double pneumonia a few years before and he is still grieving her. Or, actually, the narrator is the elderly man that the boy became and the book, he says, is "a round-about, futile way of making amends."

For what, one immediately wonders, is he "making amends"? Cletus and the narrator apparently met once in a half-finished house that was being built by the narrator's father and then played together a few times. Several years later, after the murder and suicide, they coincidentally ended up attending the same high school in Chicago. But when the narrator passed Cletus in the hall one day in that high school, he didn't say hello, basically because he felt awkward and embarrassed by the other boy's catastrophe. Maxwell writes, "I think if I had turned and walked along beside him and not said anything, it might have been the right thing to do," but "it has taken me all these years even to imagine doing that." That's it. That's what occasions the entire book—one boy didn't say hello to another in a high school hallway. But this minor failure, this gap, opens up a chasm of regret, and, indeed, a strange kind of mourning. From this failure, an intense act of imagining takes place as the narrator reconstructs the entire story of the affair and the deaths, winding the novel through the points of view of nearly everyone in the scene, including the Smiths' dog, and not least through his own point of view—his hunting through newspaper archives for the details of the case, his later years in analysis as an adult, his dreams, his throttled feelings about his own mother's death, his visits to his hometown when he is an adult, his musings about the tragedy.

Maxwell constantly reminds us that nearly everything about his narration is tentative, subjunctive, speculative. In fact, the first sentence of the book begins, "I very much doubt that I would have remembered for more than fifty years the murder of a tenant farmer I never laid eyes on if . . ." This is about as unimmediate as you can get—*I doubt that I would have if*—so on top of these being verbs of awareness, bane of the writing workshop, they're in the subjunctive—I would have remembered, thought, seen, understood. *I doubt that I would have if . . .*

And when the boys meet, they also meet, in a way, in the *if.* Maxwell makes his way toward this meeting by talking first about a very different sort of house, a Giacometti sculpture called *Palace at 4 a.m.* That house, the narrator says, always "reminds" him, as an adult, of the new house his father was building where he met Cletus, because the Giacometti, the art, is made of wood but has no walls, and at a room at the top there is "a queer-looking creature with the head of a monkey wrench" that looks like a cross between "a male ballet dancer and a pterodactyl." The palace, the house, is thirty inches high and "it is all terribly spare and strange." Then he explains how this object first formed in Giacometti's mind, and then he moves to discussing the half-built house where he met Cletus, but even this is surrounded by phrases like "I seem to remember," and "it could also be that," and then, too, he says, maybe he's just remembering a picture of the new house being built, and maybe this is a real memory or maybe it's "a form of storytelling." Only then—after the art, the artist's dream, the narrator's highly conditional memory and undermining of his own memory, do we get Cletus. Here is the scene:

> Before the stairway was in, there was a gaping hole in the center of the house and you had to use the carpenters' rickety ladder to get to the second floor. One day I looked down through this hole and saw Cletus Smith standing on a pile of lumber looking at me. I suppose I said, "Come on up." Anyway, he did.

It's sort of a miracle that Cletus is there at all after all this conditionalness, but there he is, at last, quite a real boy, framed, like a picture, by a hole in the center of the house through which the narrator sees him. The boys meet. They hang out together a bit and then the narrator tells us something else: that even though this meeting took place after the affair and the wreckage, but before the murder and suicide, and, of course, after the death of the narrator's mother, "I didn't tell Cletus about my shipwreck . . . and he didn't tell me about his." So the two boys were, in their way, two shipwrecks passing in the night, walking through this uncanny, unfinished house. Their intimacy is provisional, transitory, and not understood by either of them at the time. This scene is the entire interaction between them, plus the moment of the narrator not saying anything to Cletus in the hallway. And yet it is this fleeting encounter that occasions the entire book, a profound deployment of the narrator's imagination, a world-making intimacy.

The novel, remember, tells us an important story of its own making—the shipwreck that is one boy meeting the shipwreck that is another in the unfinished house, the cloud of truly horrible tragedy over the boy who can't tell his story, and then the impetus for the other boy telling that boy's story for him: because he failed him in life, failed to say hello to him in the hallway, failed to connect. If he had been able to so much as reach out to Cletus in that hallway, there would be no need for the book, the art, the Giacometti. But because of that "failure," that *if* that we now see is so double-edged, the narrator must build the palace that is this book, and, moreover, he is showing us that he's building it, showing us that this is all subjunctive, conditional, fragmentary, partial, invented, guilty. We sometimes talk about ironic distance in fiction, and I think that here Maxwell is achieving his ironic distance through grammar, essentially—through the subjunctive, and the subjunctive is explicitly standing on an acute sense of moral failure: If I had been able. If I had loved. If I had grieved.

In terms of structure, Maxwell is building a palace in the air midway through the book, a palace made of testimony that never happened about a murder that certainly did, the existence of which he has proved through documents—newspaper accounts, police reports. The narrator is explicitly telling us that this is probably all wrong, invented, perhaps dreamed, but he is also telling us that this is what is owed to Cletus, and that this book is a kind of reparation for a failure of empathy. What one boy has to do with one another, what is so important about this moment where they intersected, is, I think, that it is the moment when one boy became the narrator of the other via imagination. He becomes a writer, in effect. Not because he's such a good storyteller, but because he failed, because there is a gap, because we can achieve a union and a reunion, an intimacy in art that may not be possible in real life. Indeed, can one conceive of a more intimate act than to imagine the most private core of someone else's entire life as well as the interior life of his entire family, right down to the thoughts of the dog, albeit a dog that didn't actually exist?

With this book, the narrator finally imagines the other—not because Cletus was his brother or his father or his beloved or his enemy, but actually exactly the opposite—because Cletus was a stranger to him, someone whom he met in the unfinished house of mourning where we all live. The almost unbearably brief flash of recognition between them is caused not by the intimacy of love, but by the intimacy of death—they're both mourners. And the *if* that pervades the book is so ironic, in a way, because there actually isn't any *if* when it comes to death and grieving; the human mortality rate is 100 percent. So that *if* includes all of us as well, a community of mourners who can recognize ourselves in those two Midwestern boys of nearly a century ago. *Meet me in the* if. The postmodern cleverness of that invitation in the Spike Jonze film—a film, it must be said, with a profound tenderness pulsing at its core—in Maxwell is a heartbroken entreaty to the past, a letter that can be neither sent nor answered, and yet must be written; its composition seems to be a matter of profound emotional urgency.

The House in Paris, like *So Long, See You Tomorrow,* also concerns a brief crossing of young psyches that opens, and then closes, a door to the past. Two children of about ten, Henrietta and Leopold, meet for one day in a house in Paris. They are both traveling, in the company of a chaperoning spinster named Miss Fisher—Leopold has come from Italy to see his biological mother, whom he has never met; Henrietta is going from England to Mentone, in France, where she will stay with her grandmother. Henrietta's mother is dead, and her father doesn't really seem to know what to do with her; Leopold lives with adoptive parents in Italy. Both children are nervous, precocious, curious. They don't play together so much as interview one another and knock around the house, bored. And that house, like the half-built house in the Maxwell book, is odd: it's described as looking "miniature, like a doll's house," peculiarly narrow, on a street that is preternaturally silent, and inside there is "doll's house furniture." It's a sort of dream house, uncanny, a way station. Upstairs, an elderly woman, Madame Fisher, Miss Fisher's mother, is dying. The first section ends with devastating news for Leopold: his mother is not coming.

The narrative now flips back to the story of Leopold's mother, Karen. Engaged to marry a solid man named Ray, she falls in love instead with Max, the fiancé of her friend Naomi Fisher—yes, that same Miss Fisher who is now taking care of the children—and becomes pregnant by him, with Leopold. News of the affair comes out. Max is then manipulated and psychologically tormented by Madame Fisher, who is in love with him; he kills himself; Leopold is born and sent away to Italy; Karen marries Ray after all, but everyone's life is ruined. As in *So Long, See You Tomorrow*, there is a melodrama folded into the center of the book: illicit love, heartbreak, passionate death.

In the last section of the book, we go back to the present, back to the moment when Karen has not arrived to meet Leopold. As with Maxwell, you have a melodrama wrapped up by something apparently much drier and more random, the afternoon of two latchkey kids essentially, and if Cletus and Maxwell's narrator were ships, or shipwrecks, Henrietta and Leopold are basically passing trains. And, in fact, at one point Miss Fisher refers to this uncanny doll's house as "a depôt for young people crossing Paris." But the climactic scene of the book has nothing to do with the adult melodrama. Instead, it is a scene of Leopold crying because his mother hasn't come—the most natural, ordinary, unremarkable thing that a ten-year-old boy might do. But what happens here has an extraordinary intensity. Bowen gives it two full pages of its own, and most important is the fact that it is perceived through the point of view, indeed through the very body, of Henrietta.

> If it were just crying . . . thought Henrietta. . . . At first each sob was like some terrible accident, then they began to come faster. . . .

She could not know how sharply Leopold realized everything that at this moment perished for him—landscapes, his own moments, hands approaching making him unsuspicious. She had seen the country he had thought he would inherit—her certainty of it made it little, his passionate ignorance made it great—trees rounded, standing in their own shadow, spires glittering, lakes of land in light, white puffs from the little train travelling a long way. He is weeping because he is not going to England; his mother is not coming to take him there. He is weeping because he has been adopted; he is weeping because he has got nowhere to go. He is weeping because this is the end of imagination—imagination fails when there is no *now*. . . .

She watched his head, the back of his thin neck, the square blue collar shaken between his shoulders, wondering without diffidence where to put her hand. Finally, she leant her body against his, pressing her ribs to his elbow so that his sobs began to go through her too. . . . Her face bent forward, so that the tears she began shedding fell on the front of her dress. . . .

Now that she cried, he could rest. . . . Leopold, she could feel, was looking out of the window, seeing the courtyard and the one bare tree swim into view again and patiently stand.

That's the moment—the child Henrietta, like the narrator in the Maxwell book, imagines the other. She feels what he feels. She sees what he sees. She goes through the transformative door of the *if*. And once that happens, the book can be over. Which is to say, of course, that the exterior melodrama—and in both books this is long over, a done deal, it's had its climactic moments—both is and isn't the point. The point is the knowledge that comes through this empathic imagining, this *if*, and the corresponding idea that that knowledge is an essential part of growing up. Henrietta and Leopold, Cletus and Maxwell's narrator can't get out of the uncanny house of memory without it. In Bowen's novel, ten-year-old Henrietta not only imagines the other, she imagines the horror of what it would be for that other, Leopold, a motherless boy as she is a motherless girl, to come to the "end of imagination"—for a writer, this is a kind of death. The "husk of silence" around Leopold is similar to the husk of silence around Cletus Smith—in these books, the other child, the one who wasn't quite as close to the blast of the disaster, must pierce this silence, must imagine, must inhabit that silence even when, as in Maxwell, he or she feels that it may be unbearable, unsayable, nearly impossible.

The deepest and most powerful intimacy in both these extraordinary novels is an act of the imagination, explicitly, a critical embrace of the *what if,* the subjunctive, as a form of reparation: the reparation that is the book in Maxwell, the reparation that is seeing, though *seeing* is too small a word for it, from the other's point of view in Bowen—one might better say *experiencing,* knowing in the fullest sense what a tree in a courtyard looks like to a ten-year-old boy after he has come to the end of imagining and, perhaps, most important, being able to bear that visceral, emotional knowledge in one's own body and mind. Meeting in the *if,* in these two novels, disembodied as it is, provides a very powerful route to that knowledge.

Meeting in the World

That sort of visceral emotional knowledge, the pursuit of which is not valued as much as perhaps it once was on the crest of Freud, was also, of course, D. H. Lawrence's great theme, or one of them, although his route was exactly the opposite: very much through the body. For this reason, among others, we think of him, more or less, as the sometimes purplish novelist of sex. Modern readers can have a tough time with Lawrence, not so much, perhaps, with the sex per se as with the seriousness, even the portentousness, with which Lawrence treats it. Things can get a little archetypal, thematically overinflated. But Lawrence's basic belief that there is a special kind of knowledge to be gained from physical communion, and from emotions like love and desire, is worth reconsidering, not because of what it does or doesn't tell us about sex, but because Lawrence seemed to believe that the poetics of primal drives could tell us something about how to be in the world. For Lawrence, intimacy—usually, though not always, sexual intimacy between men and women—is actually not so much a way in as a way out of the prison house of self, of place, of circumstance and into a larger, even a much larger, consciousness.

Transcendence is not what Lawrence's people are endlessly seeking; it's more like profound disturbance. His working-class characters, and sometimes his characters from other classes, use their bodies to break open their psyches, to know something, get somewhere that isn't available to them by any other means. Intimacy, for Lawrence, is so serious because it is often the only boat out of a crushing psychological and cultural localness. On a philosophical level, there is not much difference between what it means to Maxwell's narrator to imagine Cletus's most private self, and to Lawrence's grown-up men and women having sexual intercourse. The intimate and consequential boundary crossings are the same, though the physical means may be quite different, or even, in Maxwell's case, when no physicality is involved at all.

With Lawrence, however, these crossings are not only personal or psychological. He suggests that, in a sort of inverse image of Courbet's famous painting *The Origin of the World,* the knowledge yielded by the intimacy of sex actually shifts the characters' openness to and knowledge not only of themselves and one or two other people, but also of the world itself—its difference, its disturbing otherness, its irrefutable and uncontrollable presence. It's a lot for sex to bear, which may be the other reason modern readers bridle against Lawrence; can intimacy be loaded down with that much existential freight? It seems naive, a possibly tragicomic mismanagement of expectations. But at the very least, what this produces in Lawrence's prose is fascinating. The Lawrence oeuvre is massive; here, I'm just going to talk about one brief section of Lawrence's novel *The Rainbow*.

In *The Rainbow*, we feel the impact of the lovers' meeting not particularly, or even at all explicitly, in their bodies; rather, we feel it as it shifts their perceptions of the world around them. The world, here, is that space between, the register and ground of the characters' primal intimacy. *The Rainbow* is the story of several generations of the working-class Brangwen family, in particular their love relationships and marriages. Throughout, it's psychologically quite astute as it tracks the dynamics of intimate relationships. But the narrative primal scene of the book, the wellspring of the powerful and complicated emotions that suffuse the book, is the desperate, demiarticulate passion that twenty-eight-year-old Tom Brangwen, born and bred in rural Nottingham, feels for a woman who is very strange to him, Anna Lensky, a Polish widow six years his elder with one child who has immigrated, uneasily, to this small English village. Upon seeing Anna for the first time, he feels not lust, and not even lust behind a discreet fig leaf of overblown imagery, but this: "He felt as if he were walking again in a far world, not Cossethay, a far world, the fragile reality." And a bit farther on: "It was to him a profound satisfaction that she was a foreigner." Brangwen is as mesmerized by Anna's foreignness as he is by her physical beauty or her personality; in her strange presence, he feels, paradoxically, more acutely himself for the first time in his life. "With her," Lawrence writes, "he would be real." The feeling is mutual, though not symmetrical—Anna is as drawn to him as he is to her, but she also fears him as someone who will require her to "find a new being, a new form."

As they fall in love, Lawrence tracks the growing intimacy between them in tremendous emotional detail. He traces every psychic ripple in language that is remarkably mutual, that somehow, continually, not only voices both their perspectives at the same time, but also shows the effect that they are having on one another. In one extraordinary sentence, Lawrence writes, "A shiver, a sickness of new birth passed over her, the flame leaped up him, under his skin." In fewer than twenty words, not only does the torch of perspective pass unremarked from her to him, but it is as if the substance of the emotion itself passes from her to him and changes form as it goes—that "shiver," that chill, that "sickness of new birth" passes over her and, syntactically, sets him on fire from the inside out, under his skin—from cold to hot, from her to him, both of them transformed, differently, but in equal measure, as if love had alchemical properties that work on human beings. It's as if there is something, some deep emotional grammar, underneath the exchange, some unimaginably primal zone where fire and ice are somehow the same, and can transmute seamlessly into one another.

In this remarkably physical image Lawrence shows the emotion communicating between them while at the same time retaining a fundamental doubleness—they are not feeling the same thing at the same time, they are not merging one into the other, they are not becoming one or even necessarily understanding one another especially well. One would not wish to be a fly on the wall during their dinner conversations. It's something else that connects them, something that includes but is not limited to sex, that has to do with but is not limited to gender difference, something that renders them each both more real and more foreign to themselves in one another's presence. They wouldn't, couldn't, be together if they weren't so fundamentally other to one another, but it is in many ways more an otherness of the soul than of the body. There's something about Anna that Tom can never quite fathom. Kissing her for the first time, he feels "something break in his brain." Lawrence writes, "He could not bear to be near her, and know the utter foreignness between them, know how entirely they were strangers to each other." Eventually, of course, he must marry her.

But in contact with that strangeness, an interesting change occurs in Tom's understanding of his position in the world. He moves from a lower order of consciousness, strictly bounded by the local, to a much broader perspective. Once Tom falls in love with Anna, Lawrence writes, when he looks at the stars at night, he "knew he did not belong to himself. He must admit that he was only fragmentary, something incomplete and subject. There were the stars in the dark heaven travelling, the whole host passing by on some eternal voyage. So he sat small and submissive to the greater ordering." The growing intimacy between Tom and Anna decenters Tom, moves him out of himself and into consciousness of a much wider world. He sees the familiar differently—not in a rosy glow of love, but reframed, recontextualized, by the always slightly unreachable consciousness of another.

Narratives of romantic love often invoke the idea of the "soul mate," a kind of amplification and reflection of one's deepest, most private self; but what Lawrence is suggesting here is that romantic love can be such a powerful experience of the other's presence, his or her soul if you will, that it expands your soul, it opens your soul to a perhaps painful, and humbling, degree. For instance, here is Lawrence's description of Anna, watching Tom come through her kitchen door to ask her to marry him: "She stood away, at his mercy, snatched out of herself. She did not know him, only she knew he was a man come for her." This is intimacy, as I said before, as disturbance, a force that wakes you up, de-centers you, radically changes your perception of the world around you and your place in it. And notice that the impact is the same for the man and the woman—they are both changed deeply, though not in the same way, by encountering one another.

Whether or not one thinks that this is possible in real life, notice the impact it has on the page. These are two characters, to move to a prosaic, workmanlike plane, who can't really talk to one another very well, barely know themselves, and actually aren't having that much sex, which Lawrence, his reputation notwithstanding, doesn't describe in graphic detail, anyway. (However, it is worth noting that *The Rainbow*, which was published in 1915, was found at a trial to be so obscene that all copies were seized and burnt. It's hardly explicit or pornographic by today's standards, but perhaps what was so distressing to the forces of censorship is that Lawrence pitched sex neither as sheer bodily urge nor as a kind of simple physical expression of the higher emotion of love; instead, he saw it as a powerful, serious force that makes its own path through people's lives, like a river. His attitude toward sex isn't titillating—indeed, it's rather grave.)

So, in order for us to feel the weight and depth of an

intimate connection that even the lovers themselves don't understand all that well, Lawrence moves to the impact this connection is having on their perceptions— again, we understand from the change in their perceptions that it's the inchoate emotion subtending the perceptions that's the driving force here, but he doesn't force his characters to be articulate about it. Instead, he finds the force of the intimacy in the delineation of a space between them literally, figuratively, and syntactically, a space that wells up that neither of them controls and that the reader understands not only as a register of the characters' connection, but also on a visceral level, directly.

In *The Rainbow,* with its emphasis on foreignness, Lawrence explicitly renders that space between as the world. Intimacy redraws the characters' map of the world and their place within it. Intimacy snatches you out of yourself, shows you how small you are in relation to the rest of the universe. Notice how different an idea this is from some of our modern clichés about love—that it should make you "feel good" about yourself, feel confident, feel attractive, feel accompanied, feel, in a sense, bigger. Here, intimacy causes the characters to feel uncertain, off-balance, strange, sometimes smaller, sometimes expanded in unexpected ways. Out walking one windy night, in love, Tom sees the world like this: "Big holes were blown into the sky, the moonlight blew

about. Sometimes a high moon, liquid-brilliant, scud-
ded across a hollow space and took cover under electric, brown-iridescent cloud-edges." If we were going
to ask Why does Tom love Anna? the answer would be:
Because she makes him feel like this, like holes have been
blown into the sky. I don't know if *romantic* is exactly
the word for this, but one certainly feels the exceptional
force of the emotion between them.

Now, in talking about Lawrence, one can't leave out
actual sex. But when he does finally produce a scene
of literal sexual intimacy, nearly everything that happens is told in the kind of double voice of the sentence I
quoted before, the one that switches perspective in the
middle. The lead-in to this scene is that Tom and Anna,
now married and with a child of their own, have had a
period of estrangement, they've been fighting, but then
they reunite in a towering two-page sex scene, which is
perhaps most notable for the fact that there are basically no bodies on the page at all. Instead, there are
quite complex and somewhat abstract images of shifts
of consciousness. Lawrence writes: "She was the door-
way to him, he to her. At last they had thrown open the
doors, each to the other, and had stood in the doorways
facing each other." It's not very sexy, really. Though,
like the extraordinary sentence I discussed earlier, it's
deeply concerned with rendering mutuality, with finding an image for a shared space of intimacy, a shared,

kinetic interiority—here, these endless doors and doorways, this face to face that is not rendered in particularly physically intimate terms.

And yet we feel not only their closeness, their reconciliation, but also so much more: that moment just as the doors are thrown open, the mutual expectation, desire, and regard. We feel both the yearning and the possibility; interestingly, in a veiled but more explicit passage just before the passage about the doorways, Lawrence writes that Tom "pressed forward, nearer, nearer. . . . If really he could be destroyed, burnt away till he lit with her in one consummation, that were supreme, supreme." But this more physical sentence is actually in the subjunctive—*if he could, if it were.* Nearer, but never quite there. I don't think this is because of some post-Victorian modesty in Lawrence, some sense of wishing to avoid the textual money shot, even one draped in lots of early-twentieth-century overwriting. He's choosing to locate the intimacy in the pressing, the seeking, the opening of the door, the shifting perceptions of the world around them.

Toward the end of this same sex scene, he writes, "The new world was discovered, it remained only to be explored." Lawrence doesn't mean the world within, or only the world within; he doesn't mean the world of sex; he means the entire world. And, in fact, after they've had this towering sexual encounter and the marriage is healed, Lawrence writes, "They did not think of each other—why should they? Only when she touched him, he knew her instantly, that she was with him, near him, that she was the gateway and the way out, that she was beyond, and that he was travelling in her through the beyond." United, and reunited, with Anna, Tom sees the world in a way that would otherwise not be possible for him. Intimacy brings a liberating knowledge of the foreign, the beyond, of the limits of the self in a much bigger universe. It's almost frightening in its power, which may be another reason modern readers look askance at Lawrence. As domestic as this situation is— it is, after all, the story of the early days of a marriage— this Lawrentian kind of intimacy feels undomesticated, dangerous, radical. It changes things at the root, it destabilizes you, hurls you into the world. As with Bowen and Maxwell, it's actually a lot to bear, and not for the faint of heart.

Meeting in the Image

Somewhere between the world itself and the possible worlds of the subjunctive is the image. It is a flexible and expansive place for characters to meet, one that doesn't even require the characters to be physically in the same room or to talk with or touch one another; they can be united in the capacious mind of the author, brought together by simile and metaphor. Though it isn't always the case and doesn't have to be, beauty is attracted to the image, or perhaps the image to beauty. Among many other things, beauty has a way of dissolving the reader's defenses, opening up a zone of possibility. In her brilliant little book *On Beauty and Being Just,* Elaine Scarry writes that "Beautiful things . . . always carry greetings from other worlds within them." The image lends itself as well to creating those other worlds, and to uniting its characters there in ways that they may not themselves even be quite aware of. Bringing characters into intimacy via a powerful image doesn't actually require their participation, nor does that intimacy, in contrast to Lawrence, Bowen, and Maxwell, have to change the characters psychologically. This use of the image is more a sort of benevolent tyrant, or maybe a guru—the image reveals an almost spiritual connectedness underneath known by the author, but not necessarily by the characters, or all the characters. It's the aquifer, the air that surrounds them, a sea of connection and interconnection.

The master, or one of the masters, of the image is Virginia Woolf. In Woolf, the image is the meeting ground for any and all human beings everywhere; it is communion, erotic space; it is transformational, a way of knowing; it's magic, capable of moving outside the confines of time and space, leaping at will from person to person. In her novel *To the Lighthouse,* there's a scene about midway through the book where everyone in the Ramsay household is at dinner together. The candles have just been lit.

> Now eight candles were stood down the table, and after the first stoop the flames stood upright and drew with them into visibility the long table entire, and in the middle a yellow and purple dish of fruit. What had she done with it, Mrs. Ramsay wondered, for Rose's arrangement of the grapes and pears, of the horny pink-lined shell, of the bananas, made her think of a trophy fetched from the bottom of the sea, of Neptune's banquet, of the bunch that hangs with vine leaves over the shoulder of Bacchus (in some picture), among the leopard skins and the torches lolloping red and gold. . . . Thus brought up suddenly into the

light it seemed possessed of great size and depth, was like a world in which one could take one's staff and climb hills, she thought, and go down into valleys, and to her pleasure (for it brought them into sympathy momentarily) she saw that Augustus too feasted his eyes on the same plate of fruit, plunged in, broke off a bloom there, a tassel here, and returned, after feasting, to his hive. That was his way of looking, different from hers. But looking together united them.

Now all the candles were lit up, and the faces on both sides of the table were brought nearer by the candle light, and composed, as they had not been in the twilight, into a party round a table, for the night was now shut off by panes of glass, which, far from giving any accurate view of the outside world, rippled it so strangely that here, inside the room, seemed to be order and dry land; there, outside, a reflection in which things wavered and vanished, waterily.

Some change at once went through them all, as if this had really happened, and they were all conscious of making a party together in a hollow, on an island; had their common cause against that fluidity out there.

Notice the engine of transformative intimacy in this passage: the agency in the scene belongs to the flames, the light that begins by drawing the table "into visibility," making it appear; almost, it seems, bringing it into existence and then adding that dish of fruit that, transformed into image in Mrs. Ramsay's mind, an image that plunges first to the bottom of the sea, then to Bacchus, then becomes an alternate world, then brings Mrs. Ramsay and Augustus together. These two characters could not be more different, "but looking together united them." The light brings the object into the world, the object as an image, a thing that one looks at—literally bringing greetings from other worlds, bringing alternate worlds alive in the mind's eye—and that seeing unites, first, two people. Then Woolf returns to that image of the candlelight, and now she moves the circle of intimacy wider—"the faces on both sides of the table were brought nearer by the candle light, and composed, as they had not been in the twilight, into a party round a table." That flame, that image, brings the people at the table together in a composition—the people themselves are not moving together; they are not necessarily experiencing this growing intimacy. The light is experiencing it; the reader is experiencing it.

And then Woolf moves the circle of intimacy wider still—"Some change at once went through them all . . . and they were all conscious of making a party together"—so now the light that has composed them wakes them up to their communion, their togetherness. They feel themselves to be united "against that fluidity out there," a fluidity that is an echo and a reflection of the fluidity inside the room, the permeability of boundaries between and among the people at the table, who are now so intimately connected that they all change "at once." Those panes of glass are all that stands between the borderless human beings inside the lighted room and the dark, wavering world outside the room—communion, in a sense, is everywhere all the time, everything is just on the verge of melting at any given moment. It's probably too bald to suggest that the border-dissolving light inside the room is eros and the border-dissolving light outside the room is thanatos—Mrs. Ramsay is, after all, just a few pages away from her death—but I think I'll make that bald suggestion anyway. We readers are naturally drawn to the light, but Woolf puts that darkness right next to it, driving us even closer to it; we are drawn into closeness with the Ramsay family as well, making a party with them against the encroaching darkness.

All of this work is being done, basically, by the image of the candlelight. No one at the table is turning to anyone else and saying, "You know, I've always wanted to tell you . . ." or holding hands or exchanging lingering glances or even thinking of one another. Woolf brings them together, and brings us together with them, in that image, which is, of course, also actual candlelight, eight candles at the table. It's not a one-to-one intimacy; it's not romantic; it's not, in a way, personal at all. And yet we feel a tremendous tenderness upon reading this scene, a welling-up of sympathy; we feel very close to the Ramsay family, as if we understand something incredibly private about them, nearly as if we're with them at a family moment when outsiders really shouldn't be there. Looking together at an image, an image that is itself mobile and perhaps appears differently to each viewer, we are united with them, and they are united with one another. What might we call this union through looking? It isn't scopophilia, although it might be called, perhaps, *scopoagape,* or brotherly love through looking—a word that doesn't exist. It may be that what I experienced at the Goldin exhibit could be described as *scopoagape,* a shared sense of visual desire, and of expressing desire via a visual image.

In his novel *The Soul Thief,* Charles Baxter creates a sense of *scopoagape* among characters and reader through his use of an image in a sex scene. The two characters having sex are an odd couple: Nathaniel, the novel's beleaguered narrator, and Jamie, a woman who generally sleeps only with women, but is having an affair with Nathaniel. Baxter writes,

> Half an hour later, his eyes closed, then suddenly opened, tears and sweat dripping down onto her, he calls out her name, and in response Jamie comes at

the same time that he does. Her facial expression is one of pleasure mixed with horrified surprise. After a moment—she has broken out into quick shocked laughter—he looks into her eyes and imagines that her spirit, without knowing how or why, has suddenly disobeyed the force of gravity that has governed it. Her soul, no longer a myth but now a fact, ascends above her body. Like a little metallic bird unused to flight, unsteady in its progress, her soul rises and falls, frightened by the heights and by what it sees, but excited, too, by being married to him for a few seconds, just before it plummets back to earth.

Jamie, it should be said, is an artist and the image of the metallic bird here is also a reference to the metallic birds she makes herself. Nathaniel knows her work, so that's why the image comes to his mind—it's not just randomly pretty. So this, obviously, is an ordinary intimacy, the intimacy of lovers for however brief a time, and they're doing a recognizably intimate thing, nothing fancy. The image, like that image of the candlelight, is beautiful, it's lyrical—the soul in flight, a bird; as a description of orgasm, it's lovely and it goes very far out of its way to cede the floor to her, imagistically speaking; Nathaniel, wide awake, is busy not thinking of his own soul, but imagining hers in detail. He is a gentleman, undoubtedly, though one senses that he might be possibly a tiny bit pleased, secretly, that her soul, apparently "unused to flight," has been released from the heavy hand of gravity by having sex with him.

The lovers are united in the image, first, by the fact that this is Nathaniel looking at Jamie and imagining her, making an image of her most intimate experience of herself, in the same way that Maxwell's narrator imagined Cletus Smith or Henrietta imagined Leopold. He sees that bird, a much more intimate thing than seeing her naked, having sex with her, even coming with her. He is actually able to see, and make a metaphor of, her experience of her own soul. But also embedded, even somewhat hidden in the image of the bird in flight is an equally powerful insight into Nathaniel. Watch what happens: the bird is rising, "frightened by the heights and by what it sees, but excited, too, by being married to him for a few seconds."

This is syntactically complicated; we must look closely to discern the subtle, inverted image. Baxter reverses the literal positions of the lovers not in physical space, but in psychic space—within the image that Nathaniel conceives of Jamie's soul. When the passage begins, Nathaniel's sweat is dripping down onto Jamie, so he's on top, but in the image she, as that metallic bird, a soul, is looking down at him, she is seeing him and in that seeing she is "married to him"; in other words, in her pleasure, the pleasure he gives her and that they have together, she recognizes him, she sees him, they are united in her gaze from above. It is a moment of transcendent intimacy for both of them, very brief, "a few seconds," before that plummet back to earth, but that flight she takes isn't only for her pleasure—it's so that, from her vantage point, he might actually be seen, be "married"; the powerful intimate gaze, here, the gaze that unites, is mutual. It's almost as if the narrative lofts Jamie's soul so high in order for her to look down at Nathaniel and see him whole, see him from a point of view that no human being actually could see from, an encompassing, aerial, almost divine point of view.

Again, this is subtle, mostly off the page, but if you follow the logic of the image it's easy to see that, gentleman though he is, Nathaniel isn't as self-effacing as he might seem. His desire is bound up in that image as well, and also, of course, his loss: the plummet back to earth. The recognition he has so desired, that he has worked so hard for and that came off so well, so lyrically, even beautifully, lasts for only a few seconds. It's post-Lawrentian in terms of explicitness, but also post-Lawrentian in terms of the optimism, or lack thereof, about what this particular kind of intimacy can do—sex and desire do have a ferocious, disturbing power, but only for a moment or so now and then. Inevitably, the moment passes, both the decentering and the marriage are brief, the characters remain local, citizens only of their own skins.

Meeting in the Dark

Up to this point, I have been discussing intimacies in fiction that might be more or less described as emanating from eros—the life instinct, the generative force. In Bowen, Maxwell, Lawrence, Woolf, and Baxter, the space between is a creative one, producing art and insight and communion. However, the space between can also emanate from thanatos—the death drive, the destructive force. The intimacy that can seam can also rend, and the writer's task is similar: to draw readers into that dark space and to persuade them of its meaning and its gravity. If the reader, in the novels that I've discussed so far, is a seduced voyeur, an invisible participant in these scenes of union and expansion of consciousness, in other, darker fictions, the reader is drawn into complicity with intimacies that may well do harm. Moreover, the harm may lie not only in the literal action on the page, but also in the reader's very engagement with that harm, with the act of reading itself. It means one thing to spy on a scene of love of whatever variety, but what might it mean to spy on a scene of intimate destruction? Are readers implicated by their desire to turn the pages? One method by which writers create a space between in which to do intimate damage is the use of blur, penumbra, and darkness. Under cover of syntactical and literal twilight, crimes take place, often in such a way that it can be difficult to discern, at first glance, that a crime has taken place at all.

In Joseph Conrad's *The Secret Sharer,* unsettling questions of power and identity are intricately folded into a yarn that is also a strange love story, and a story about the love of strangeness itself, of the stranger within and of strange lives unlived. The shimmering, almost over-determined homoeroticism of *The Secret Sharer* should not entirely blind us to the fact that, as much as this is a novella about a liminal love, it is also a novella about a murder, a splitting, a forceful and conscious subduing as one man literally masters another in order to consti-tute his own authority. That the man who is ultimately subdued is himself a murderer should alert us to what kind of topos this is: a deadly one, in which power is a zero-sum game.

The plot of *The Secret Sharer,* which is less than fifty pages long, is fairly simple: an unnamed sea captain, embarking on his first commission in the Gulf of Siam on an unnamed ship, harbors a fugitive sailor named Leggatt who has more than likely murdered a man on a nearby vessel, the *Sephora.* The captain stashes Leggatt in his rooms on the ship; over the course of a few days, the two men develop a deep, secret intimacy; the captain feels that Leggatt is his double both literally and psychologically; he hides Leggatt from the authorities, risking his own commission; in the climactic final scene, the captain sails perilously close to an island in order to enable Leggatt's escape. Watching Leggatt swim away, the captain feels that "the secret sharer of my cabin and of my thoughts, as though he were my second self, had lowered himself into the water to take his punishment: a free man, a proud swimmer striking out for a new destiny."

It's a curious sentence, tacking paradoxically between self and other, punishment and freedom, longing and rejection. That it is the final sentence of the book is more curious still, and only increases the sense of ambivalence in the main character and unease in the reader. What, exactly, has happened between these two men? What "secret" has passed between them?

This scene of Leggatt swimming for freedom in the water echoes the scene in which the captain first discovers Leggatt, lurking just beneath his ship:

> The side of the ship made an opaque belt of shadow on the darkling glassy shimmer of the sea. But I saw at once something elongated and pale floating very close to the ladder. Before I could form a guess a faint flash of phosphorescent light, which seemed to issue

suddenly from the naked body of a man, flickered in the sleeping water with the elusive, silent play of summer lightning in a night sky. With a gasp I saw revealed to my stare a pair of feet, the long legs, a broad livid back immersed right up to the neck in a greenish cadaverous glow. One hand, awash, clutched the bottom rung of the ladder. He was complete but for the head. A headless corpse! . . . He raised up his face, a dimly pale oval in the shadow of the ship's side. But even then I could only barely make out down there the shape of his black-haired head. However, it was enough for the horrid, frost-bound sensation which had gripped me about the chest to pass off. . . .

As he hung by the ladder, like a resting swimmer, the sea lightning played about his limbs at every stir; and he appeared in it ghastly, silvery, fishlike. He remained as mute as a fish, too. He made no motion to get out of the water, either.

Later, when the captain is hiding Leggatt in his small cabin belowdecks, Leggatt is described in similarly non-human, sometimes corpselike or wraithlike, terms. He is "glimmering white"; he appears from out of a closet without making a sound; he is "noiseless as a ghost"; he holds entirely still as he stands against the wall in small spaces, "his face looking very sunken in daylight, his eyelids lowered," like a corpse propped upright; he is prone to vanishing; the captain even wonders at one point if Leggatt is visible to others. Indeed, when Leggatt is speaking of his forthcoming escape by sea, he remarks, "It would never do for me to come to life again. . . . As I came at night so I shall go."

The recurrent image of Leggatt as glimmering, shimmering, silvery, mute, and still, uncannily poised between the animate and the inanimate, is, of course, an image of a reflection in a mirror. The captain constantly reinforces this image by seeing Leggatt as his double, his twin, his second self. In the long passage quoted here, the position of the captain as Leggatt raises his face up is akin to the position of a man looking at his reflection in water; like a reflection in water, Leggatt's face, "upturned exactly" under the captain's, is blurry, a "dimly pale oval." More than once, the captain confides that, with Leggatt hidden in his cabin, he frequently feels "in two places at once" and only feels "less torn in two when I [am] with him."

However, there is little on the page to suggest that Leggatt is literally the captain's double either physically or psychologically. The reader is told, repeatedly, by the captain, that Leggatt is the captain's double, but the work of this doubling is done by the continual mirror positioning of the two men more than by any articulated attributes. The captain even remarks at one point, "He was not a bit like me, really." When we read the long account given by Leggatt of his violent rage on the *Sephora* during a storm, a rage that resulted in another sailor's death, we infer that the captain must harbor such a rage himself because of the curious blankness of his own inner life. Leggatt's guilt points to a similar sense of guilt somewhere in this preternaturally quiet captain. Neither the captain nor his ship is named in the story; the captain never describes himself physically. Of the two, the captain is actually the far more shadowy figure, the ghost. Leggatt is merely a man. Conrad relies on the reader to make the obvious connections that the captain is unwilling to make, even as he finds himself so powerfully drawn to Leggatt. Leggatt—named, seen, clearly marked out in every way, naked—must, by analogy, be the notably unvoiced, invisible interior of the captain. Who is this elusive captain, we wonder, what secrets is he hiding, and why is he so overidentified with Leggatt, so determined to see his own reflection in a man who may or may not be "a bit like" him at all? Why does he, in the discovery passage quoted here, put his head, visually, on Leggatt's "headless" body? But then again, why does the passage remove Leggatt's head in the first place?

We might also ask why Conrad so carefully dims the lights. The topos of *The Secret Sharer* is, literally, the dark. The men first meet at night; they "whisper together" in the captain's bed all night; when Leggatt makes his escape, it is at night. Throughout, the novella is penumbral, hushed, full of shadows and odd flashes of light, glimpses, nighttime nakedness in the sea, whispers, hidden spaces. The images are appealing to eye and ear: silky, luminescent, dusky. More often than not, Leggatt is wearing the captain's pajamas, his "sleeping suit," an image as cozy as it is sexual. Complementing and amplifying this darkness is Conrad's use of blur. Consider, for example, the very first sentence: "On my right hand there were lines of fishing stakes resembling a mysterious system of half-submerged bamboo fences, incomprehensible in its division of the domain of tropical fishes, and crazy of aspect as if abandoned forever by some nomad tribe of fishermen now gone to the other end of the ocean; for there was no sign of human habitation as far as the eye could reach." This sentence seems almost willfully confusing and difficult to parse visually. Whose right hand? The fishing stakes—staked into what, we aren't quite sure—resemble bamboo fences, which, if they were there (which they aren't) are "incomprehensible," "crazy," "abandoned" by a nomad tribe, which doesn't exist, but which isn't in the scene, anyway, because there is "no sign of human habitation" in this place, whatever it might be.

A sentence farther on, our narrator continues his obfuscating description: "And when I turned my head to take a parting glance at the tug which had just left us anchored outside the bar, I saw the straight line of the flat shore joined to the stable sea, edge to edge, with a perfect and unmarked closeness, in one leveled floor half brown, half blue under the enormous dome of the sky." Here, the sea is "stable" (the last quality that the sea might be said to possess), and it is seamlessly joined to the shore, the two elements, edgeless, boundaryless, in "a perfect and unmarked closeness." As with the scene where Leggatt appears, naked and phosphorescent and headless, floating by the side of the ship, this opening scene seems to go out of its way to displace the reader visually, to blur geography, as the earlier scene blurred anatomy, nearly to the point of illegibility. One can easily miss the radical, even surgical, operations behind the shimmering language. In fact, heads do not travel so easily back and forth from body to body, nor do the shore and sea generally meet in straight, flat, stable, perfectly unmarked planes. Quite the opposite. Often defying logic and the rules of time and space, the novella is continually in a state of whisper and blur, of small, confusing interiors that seem to have oddly endless entrances and exits; and/or of large landmasses that both by day and by night appear to be indistinguishable from the sea.

It is tremendously appealing. Conrad turns the reader round and round in the half-dark, shining lights here and there unpredictably, whispering secrets the reader can't hear, making the reader complicit in the captain's literally closeted double life, blending sea and shore and sky, shredding individual identity in a looking-glass world of misperception shadowed by offstage violence and demirepressed sexuality. The captain's unnamed ship is a dream, a cozy, erotic liminal zone where both appearance and disappearance are deceptive and unstable. Moreover, by asking the reader to contemplate a first-person narrator as obviously repressed and unreliable as the captain—he won't even tell us his name—Conrad blurs the boundaries as well between reader and narrator, inviting us to fill in so much that the captain can't or won't admit; to, in effect, write the secret history of the main character ourselves. This, too, is tremendously appealing both to the intelligence and to the heart, and we willingly connect the blurry, luminous dots. We like being party to the captain's secrets; we delight in the subterfuge, in the sly, graceful manner that Leggatt slips around the captain's cabin, undetected by the authorities.

And yet that very pleasure is perhaps both our and the captain's undoing. Conrad so beguiles us with all the ways that Leggatt gives everyone the slip that we continue that enchantment right through to the end, merrily waving Leggatt off as he jumps overboard into a nighttime sea next to an island that may well be uninhabited. It feels so much like a certain kind of happy ending ("a free man, a proud swimmer") that we can easily bounce right past the other aspect ("his punishment") of this ambiguous gesture, even though Conrad is not concealing it from us. The captain, in risking so much to secure the other man's freedom, also consolidates his previously shaky authority as his crew stands in awe of his nautical daredevilry, while simultaneously dispatching the evidence of his much more peculiar, ambivalent, erotic, murderous urges. Leggatt looks, textually, like a double, but he functions narratively and thematically as a scapegoat. Having first removed Leggatt's head and transformed him via metaphor, albeit lovely metaphor, into a corpse; dressed the other man in his own "sleeping suit," the suit in which he dreams; and loaded Leggatt up with projections of his own unruly emotions, the captain then arranges to have Leggatt willingly throw himself overboard and make of the captain a hero. Leggatt was never his double; the captain tells us that himself. Leggatt was, instead, a fugitive opportunity, an unwitting actor in the captain's intrapsychic drama, a drama that the captain orchestrates straight through to its conclusion: Leggatt's disappearance, which is not entirely unlike a suicide by drowning. "It had been a confounded lonely time," remarks Leggatt early on of his relief at being found by the captain. "I wanted to be seen, to talk with somebody, before I went on." The captain's response to this confidence is to tell Leggatt to get into his bed, where the captain is struck by how closely Leggatt resembles him.

Why this response to Leggatt's desire to "be seen"? Would we really call this love? And what of our pleasure—which surely can't be that secret to us—in watching one man co-opt, dominate, and dispatch another into exile, if not death? Where do we really think Leggatt is going? The space between, in *The Secret Sharer*, is a transactional one in which the shadow side of one character is sewn, Peter Pan–style, to the heels of another. Our suspicions might be raised by how frequently our narrator insists that he and Leggatt are just alike, are twins, are doubles, nearly to the point of suggesting that there can hardly be need of two of the same man in the world. But so beguiled are we by the atmosphere, the dusk, the whispering, and the general air of exceptional, privileged intimacy that we don't think to question why the captain is selling us on this so hard. We are lulled by the near-dark, seduced by our own cleverness in articulating what the captain refuses to articulate about himself, reading clues off of Leggatt's body.

But are we thereby overlooking the far more raw, more violent, more troubling truth hiding in plain sight? This is a tale that ends with the freshly reinscribed authority of one man and the disappearance of the other man. It seems less, at the end of the day, a story of identification than it is a story of psychological cannibalism.

Mastery comes at a price: the price is Leggatt's life and a state of permanent anonymity. The man who wanted to be seen will never be seen again.

Published in 1929, not long after *The Secret Sharer* but grounded in a very different setting, is Nella Larsen's *Passing*, which also concerns a troubled and troubling identification within a romantic friendship. The reader inhabits the point of view of one of the friends, Irene Redfield, an African American woman living with her husband and two sons in perfect respectability in a Harlem town house, patron and participant in a vibrant African American cultural scene. The object of Irene's anxiety, envy, disapproval, and admiration is her childhood friend Clare Kendry, who disorders Irene's adult life and troubles her ideas about race, identity, and desire. When the two women unexpectedly cross paths in a Chicago hotel tearoom after many years apart, their childhood friendship is reignited. Clare, Irene quickly discovers, has been passing as white for much of her life and is married to an unabashedly racist white man who doesn't know Clare's secret. At the same time, Irene begrudgingly admits to herself that she is fascinated by Clare, and Clare confesses to feeling lonely for the company of other black people, marooned, passing (she calls it "this pale life of mine") in an all-white milieu. When Clare turns up in New York and insinuates herself not only into Irene's life, but also into Irene's marriage, emotional chaos ensues for Irene.

In a highly ambiguous final scene at a party, Clare goes out a window to her death; did she fall, or did Irene push her? Neither the text nor Irene can say. "What happened next," writes Larsen of the millisecond before Clare's fall, "Irene Redfield never afterwards allowed herself to remember. Never clearly. One moment Clare had been there, a vital glowing thing, like a flame of red and gold. The next she was gone." As with the unnamed captain and Leggatt, the main character, Irene, is fascinated, seduced, and profoundly disturbed by the intruder, and she can only reestablish her identity by the death, or perhaps the murder, of the one who causes her such ambivalence and doubt, the one who brings with her "the menace of impermanence." Unlike *The Secret Sharer*, which closes on a moment that seems to be victorious, *Passing* ends with Irene passing out, overcome by a "great heaviness that submerged and drowned her. . . . Then everything was dark." She has reconsolidated herself, and vanquished the menace of impermanence, at a high price both to herself and to Clare.

Passing is a difficult novel to analyze, not least because its attitude toward its own ambiguities is so ambiguous. Is the novel as unconscious of Irene's demirepressed feelings about Clare as Irene is? If so, why plant the rather large, damning hint that Irene pushed

Clare out the window, or at the very least had an over-whelming desire to do so? If the novel is skeptical of Irene's righteousness, and open to puzzling over the contingency of identity, how does the reader square that with a final gesture that is so punitive toward its passing character? Why must Clare die to restore the marital and social order, and what does the novel think about this apparent narrative necessity? Like a passing person, the book can be seen simultaneously in several different ways depending on who's looking, what the reader's assumptions are, and what larger interests might be at stake. And like *The Secret Sharer, Passing* keeps a few cards up its sleeve, cards that slip, all but unnoticed, between its two main characters, who find so much of themselves in one another's eyes. The inti-macy between Clare and Irene is as alluring as it is ulti-mately fatal, literally to Clare and figuratively to Irene. The homoeroticism at play here need not beguile us into ignoring the fight to the death for psychic survival at the core of the novel.

Larsen, like Conrad, deploys blur, but, unlike Conrad, who creates a visual and sonic atmosphere of dimness, whisper, and soft glow, Larsen blurs the two women at the root: point of view. Irene is the close third, control-ling perspective of the novel; we only see Clare through her (often narrowed) eyes. We get Clare's backstory, her childhood, and her current concerns strictly via Irene's point of view. Clare is rarely given the opportunity to narrate her own life or to step outside of Irene's voicing of her. Even the long letter that Irene receives from Clare at the start of the novel is summed up in a few short, incomplete quotes that don't challenge Irene's idea that Clare must be, should be, miserable. As the critic Mae Henderson writes in the critical foreword to the Modern Library edition of the novel, "Metaphorically, Clare's interiority is a gap within the text; her inner life (including her hidden identity) remains sealed in the envelope, whose contents (like Clare herself) are later destroyed by Irene." The very tightness of this perspectival structure is so overdetermined that one tends to tilt toward a belief in Larsen's skepticism about her main character's hyperrespectability and its cost.

At the same time, and complicating any conclusions about what Larsen may have been up to, is this interesting aspect concerning point of view: when Irene first reencounters Clare in the hotel tearoom in Chicago, she, too, is passing. In fact, Irene, not recognizing Clare at first and assuming that the other woman is white, finds herself the object of Clare's gaze, her "strange languorous eyes," eyes that, Irene fears, see what she's hiding, because she was in search of a cool drink on a hot day and, moreover, hated "the idea of being ejected from any place." As the two women stare one another down over their respective tea services, the perspective of the novel is momentarily undone by the power of Clare's gaze. Clare, here, knows Irene, and knows that she's black and passing for white, but Irene doesn't, for several pages, recognize Clare, nor does she know that the other woman is black, and passing, as well. Who, in this moment, knows what about whom? Very oddly, by the time they're paying the bill, Clare has taken on the mantle of the passing woman, while Irene's casual slip over the color line goes unremarked by the two women, and, from here on out, by the novel as well, which seems to forget about it as rigorously as its characters do.

But can the reader? In this opening scene, the reader is drawn sweetly and firmly into Irene's pleasure, first, at being in the tearoom (it was "like being wafted upward on a magic carpet to another world"), and, soon after, at the sight of Clare: "a sweetly scented woman in a fluttering dress of green chiffon whose mingled pattern of narcissuses, jonquils, and hyacinths was a reminder of pleasantly chill spring days." Irene is immediately fascinated by this woman, not realizing that she already knows her, but she is unsettled, "put out" by the intensity of Clare's gaze at her, which is "that of one who with utmost singleness of mind and purpose was determined to impress firmly and accurately each detail of Irene's features upon her memory for all time."

A quiet duel of mutual gazing ensues for the next few pages, in which it is unclear whose looking will organize the scene, and, possibly, the narrative itself. Will Clare tell Irene's story? Or will Irene tell Clare's? Irene, who for the rest of the novel represents good race consciousness and pride, is determined, in these few moments, not to be revealed as being African American. Holding Clare's gaze, she thinks, "Suppose the woman did know or suspect her race. She couldn't prove it." The reader is off balance in this tense scene, not knowing quite whom to trust or what, exactly, is at stake.

The tension breaks when Clare crosses the room to remind Irene that they were childhood friends. From this moment on, Irene becomes firmly ensconced as the guiding perspective, and she delivers Clare's backstory— wrong side of the tracks, bad janitor dad, suspiciously fancy clothes, often seen in the company of white people—as a tale of a girl gone wrong, a pretty girl ("almost too good-looking") who can't be trusted. Girls like that, the reader knows, die a lot in novels. We are relieved, kind of, to leave the hall of mirrors where two passing women stare at one another in a segregated space, each daring the other to blow her cover, for the shelter of Irene's point of view. Irene, we see, will tell the story: Irene is black; so is Clare; Clare is a liar; liars die. Only Irene's husband, Brian, who, we later find out, is sleeping with Clare, seems capable of intuiting what

Clare's motives, her narrative drive, might be. In a discussion with Irene about Clare's racist husband and what the attraction might be, Brian remarks, "They always come back." (The "they" is somewhat ambiguous; he seems to mean white men going after black women, but in the context it could also mean black women returning to racist white men.) When Irene asks why, Brian replies, "If I knew that, I'd know what race is." It's a fascinating, telling remark that flickers past all too quickly, but leaves a strong trace. What Brian suggests is that race is as much a story lived out in the most intimate realms of one's life as it is a physical reality, and that both are ultimately unknowable. Irene quickly snaps back, "Well, Clare can just count me out," a statement that seems patently false, since the entire novel is occasioned by Clare.

Unlike *The Secret Sharer*, which seams the disappearance of Leggatt so tightly into a discourse of freedom and mastery that one almost can't see the stitches, *Passing* seems at times to be inviting the reader to consider the story being told from the point of view of the character who occupies the center of the novel, but is also silenced by it. Leggatt and the captain may or may not be at all alike; Clare and Irene, we know with certainty, are two sides of the same light-skinned coin. One woman chooses to pass; the other eschews it (except when it's convenient); both pay. In the space between them, a space as thin as a coin edge, is a vast, nearly unsayable realm of uncertainty and pain about the nature of identity itself in a racist culture. Irene reflects bitterly at one point that "Clare Kendry cared nothing for the race. She only belonged to it," a sentiment that it is probably safe to say no white character has ever uttered in a novel. Clare's freedom is as uncontainable by the book as it is by the strictures of Irene's upright consciousness, and out the window she goes.

But even here, the book seems to undercut the surface morality with image and perspective: a window, after all, is a symbol of openness and escape, and Irene is both the only character who knows exactly what happened in that moment and the one who is entirely unable to remember it. "That beauty that had torn at Irene's placid life," writes Larsen, is permanently gone. While it may be erased from Irene's life, the beauty of Clare is certainly not gone from the perspective of the reader, whom Larsen definitively separates from Irene's point of view in this scene. As in the tearoom scene, we do not trust Irene, and we, perhaps, wonder what Clare might have seen in the other woman's face as she hurtled toward the earth. There is at least one other novel in that gaze, a countertale, and the blur that creates *Passing* is also the blur that undoes any definitive reading of it. Is there a world, Larsen asks via Irene's obviously repressive stance, in which Clare doesn't have to die? The fact that Irene held the other woman for a time in her thoughts suggests that there is, but the fact that Irene then wished to erase her suggests that there isn't; the reader remains uncertainly suspended between the two.

Nearly a century after Conrad and Larsen, many veils are off. It would be difficult in modern times to pull off the kind of subtle and sublimated homoeroticism, the deep sense of unknowable mystery, that suffuses *The Secret Sharer*; it would be equally difficult for a modern reader to overlook the rather massive intrusion of Irene's subconscious and repressed desires in her relationship with Clare. We know too much, or we think we do, about what love is. We know it's a battlefield. And yet, in Dennis Cooper's piercing 1982 story "My Mark" (Cooper later revised and expanded this into the novella *Safe*, published in 1985), we see that a thanatopic intimacy can still have great power in fiction. The homoeroticism is frank—"My Mark" is the account by a man of his obsession with his ex-lover Mark—but the "death" of the other, of Mark, is not a literal death; it might be something closer to a slow dissection, and the instrument of this dissection is not a knife, but language. "My Mark" accomplishes the extraordinary feat of skinning someone alive, a former lover, through description. There is no physical violence in the story, only a gaze—and a gaze from within the imagination at that—so searching, so thorough, and so invasive that one feels slightly guilty reading it, like the worst sort of voyeur. One feels, inarticulately and inchoately, complicit with a tremendous darkness, but it is impossible to locate or account for that complicity since one is, after all, simply reading a short story. Anger at a rejecting ex-lover is nothing new. Moreover, as in Maxwell's *So Long, See You Tomorrow,* Cooper makes it clear that nearly everything we're reading in his account of Mark has been invented by the narrator. Where could the harm actually lie?

And yet.

"My Mark" begins with the bland sentence "Mark stands in the windy darkness outside a nightclub." He's been drinking, snorting coke; he throws up, falls to his knees; a man passing by helps him up, then takes him home. Drunken, stinking, sweaty, Mark nevertheless agrees to sex. "His ass," the narrator recounts, "may as well be a new best seller, the way the man thumbs to its dirty part." The description of the sex that follows is more memento mori than lusty brief encounter, stringing Mark up on his own body.

> The man grapples forward and locates a skull in
> Mark's haircut. He picks out the rims of the caves for
> his eyeballs and ears. The lantern jaw fastens below

them, studded with teeth. He comes to the long
shapely bones in Mark's shoulders, toying with them
until two blades resembling manta rays swim on the
surface. . . . He strokes through a reef of wild femurs
which keep up the ass. . . .

Mark hears the man cum. Okay, so that's over. . . .
The man grabs and kisses the apparatus on its lips.
Then he lowers his bony companion down to the floor.
It just lies there.

It isn't until midway through the story that the first-
person narrator reveals himself and reveals that he's
been narrating all along. He slips into a scene that at
first doesn't seem to include him, a moment of Mark
leaning against a wall, "his black curly hair closely
shorn." The narrator remarks, "Last year it was long. He
still seemed angelic. . . . I felt like I was on something,
but had a hard-on; the best of both worlds." Blurring
perspective, time, and even his own consciousness,
the narrator unmasks himself in the equivalent of a
mumbled aside, making himself a shadow to his ex-
lover; or, as he puts it, "a ghoul . . . dreaming of someone I barely know." If Conrad used blur and penumbra
to charm and disorient the reader while dispatching
the disturbing other into the sea, and Larsen blurred
perspective at the root so that one woman could take

ownership of the story of the disturbing other, Cooper uses shadow, blur, and a nearly entirely effaced narrator to slip up behind this Mark, this mark on the page, and describe him to death.

As we come to understand that we are reading a spurned lover's version of another man's life, specifically the other man's sex life, the reason for the malice, the invocation of Mark as skeleton, in these descriptions seems to become clear. "A man," observes the narrator, "has his face in Mark's ass. It smells like a typical one, but belongs to a boy who's a knock-out, so it's symbolic. . . . It's the end of their day, the beginning of mine. He'd just be spreading his ass with his hands and fitting it over my face about now, if he were smart and didn't need money, settled for gold in the eyes of a guy who is gaga for him."

In other words, in the ex-lover's gaze, Mark is a stupid whore, an It, a skeleton, an "apparatus" mainly identifiable by the ordinary smell of his ordinary ass. "I exaggerated his power, as it was a time in my life when I needed to feel very strongly," opines the narrator. "Mark filled the bill." This spiteful take on Mark would not be interesting, though, if Cooper didn't also allow us to see the deeper motive for this rage, that it is revenge for an injury he feels that Mark inflicted on him, but not the injury of leaving. Yes, Mark did pass as quickly through the narrator's life as he had through the lives of other men, but the injury he inflicted on the narrator was inflicted when they were together.

The narrator writes, "When I was with him his looks left me speechless, and that kind of beauty is insular, fills all my words anyway, so that what I construct must divide him from them in slight ways, such as the warmth of his skin against clinical language, like that of a man who lies down on a sharp bed of nails and is saved from real pain by the evenness of the impression." And a bit later on, "A head that has power over me. . . . I fill a head with what I need to believe about it. It's a mirage created by beauty built flush to a quasi-emotion that I'm reading in at the moment of impact."

What Cooper seems to be describing is that moment of impact, of being thrown into crisis by Mark's beauty, left "speechless," finding that his words are filled by it, that he was in some sense sealed in, because "that kind of beauty is insular." It is specifically against that speechlessness, he tells us, that he must divide "him from them"—i.e., divide Mark from his words—in order, following the logic, not to be subsumed and rendered silent by a beauty for which he was unprepared, a beauty that threw him into crisis as a man and, perhaps even more threateningly, as a writer. In self-defense, against that beautiful head with its overwhelming power, the narrator will "fill a head with what I need to believe about it." He will, in other words, reinvent Mark in his own words, render that head a skull, shroud and seal the other man in language. He will write this story that imagines Mark from the inside out, literally down to his very bones.

One feels that the piece is as much an exorcism as a work of fiction. An eye for an eye, speech for speechlessness: this is the writer's revenge, not against abandonment, but against a beauty that went to his core. "I'd loved Mark, found that emotion was possible," he writes at the end, having utterly vivisected Mark, and, perhaps, himself. The shudder that the reader may feel comes not from experiencing the ex-lover's rage at being abandoned—a very ordinary and comprehensible emotion—but from the writer's will to overwrite the other, to kill that organic, unwilled, languageless beauty with composition. Against the warmth of skin, "clinical language."

The modern writer is hard-pressed to toss characters overboard or out of windows. Instead, he delivers the blow to an ego-threatening intimacy with language. If the ego stakes in *The Secret Sharer* are mastery, and the ego stakes in *Passing* are identity, in "My Mark" the ego stakes are language itself and the ability to speak. It is fitting, in Cooper's story, that the murder is a murder in language only, that the writer makes the threatening other disappear into words. Visual beauty will not triumph over linguistic ruthlessness. For the reader, however, the shudder we feel at the end of "My Mark" is as visceral as it is in the two other texts. We know that something has gone missing, something both dearly loved and deeply feared by the narrator, who will now never be able to get it back.

Why Meet?

This is not a frivolous question. In her 1997 collection of essays *The End of the Novel of Love,* the critic Vivian Gornick makes the provocative argument that the pursuit of love is, essentially, empty as the foundation for a serious work of art. She writes that "for a hundred and fifty years in the West the idea of romantic love had been emblematic of the search for self-understanding: an influence that touched every aspect of the world enterprise." But now, she continues, apparently after the sixties, we're over it: "We loved once, and we loved badly. We loved again, and again we loved badly. We did it a third time, and we were no longer living in a world free of experience. We saw that love did not make us tender, wise, or compassionate. . . . Within ourselves we remained unchanged." She reports that "romantic love now seems a yearning to dive down into feeling and come up magically changed; when what is required for the making of a self is the deliberate pursuit of consciousness. Knowing *this* to be the larger truth, as many of us do, the idea of love as a means of illumination—in literature as in life—now comes as something of an anticlimax." She concludes, "Today, I think, love as a metaphor is an act of nostalgia, not of discovery."

To this argument, one might be tempted to reply, echoing Gornick's high-handed tone, "Speak for yourself, lady." Whose expectation is it that love only makes one "tender, wise, or compassionate"? That it is a "yearning" to be "magically changed"? Whose idea is it, moreover, that the pursuit of romantic love—as just one form of intimacy—is primarily a means of changing the self, of "self-understanding," as opposed to, say, loving another human being, or several? Gornick also repeatedly elides love, heterosexuality, and marriage as a seamless, proscriptive whole. By "love," she means: men and women getting married or getting unmarried, a definition as naive as it is offensive. That the rise of divorce in Western culture in the latter half of the twentieth century didn't deliver transformation and transcendence to the population at large seems to have led Gornick to dismiss the whole topic for art, for everyone, forever. Her idea that "many of us" have realized "the larger truth" that love is nostalgia is so sour and narcissistic as to be absurd. Gornick's stance saddens me, because it sacks love as a Great Theme on account of its inability, apparently, to deliver freedom and a bigger self; to, in other words, produce the ideals of the Enlightenment in individuals. Gornick has never, apparently, considered the possibility that this Western construct of the past few centuries might be as contingent and partial as any other construct. Instead, she blames love for being unable to measure up.

Gornick's argument does, however, inadvertently point to a different dilemma, which is the ubiquitousness, the cheapness even, of intimacy as a modern ideal. If intimacy were a person, he or she might be tired, dragged in as s/he is to glue together every sagging plot, every movie at the movieplex, every self-help book ever written, every conversation (overheard on the subway: "I know he wants to call, so I'm giving him that space"), every commercial, and many works of literary fiction. A particularly modern, faux-sincere, kitsch intimacy sells everything from afternoon talk shows to pictures on Instagram to Facebook's endlessly mined personal information, so glittering to retailers. We are continually willing to buy access to some inner zone or other, to the truth, the inside story, the "unretouched photo." But as Charles Baxter has put it, "Intimacy suggests a possibly sexualized, private, almost sacred location or space, a closeness *that not everyone can share.*" To which the average marketer might reply, "So you mean a limited edition kind of thing?" In this climate, intimacy could not be faulted for wanting to take a damn rest. And it's a bit suspicious, this reliance on intimacy as the sine qua non of human existence, it's a bit, well, thin. That's what we're down to, here in the third millennium? Spiritual enlightenment, transcendence, courage, ethics, what language is, the collective good, and, for that matter, the existence of evil: when did they become chopped liver?

I suppose we could blame modernism for making those categories so problematic that all we have left to talk about with any seriousness is human connection and its vicissitudes. And yet what we talk about when we talk about intimacy in literature is, very often, how it isn't working out, a condition we tend to agree is sad. This is the problematic truism of writing fiction today, if nothing else: the reader does not have to be convinced that intimacy matters, that intimacy always suffices for what we call the "stakes" of a story. It's not that we all necessarily believe without exception in love as salvation or enlightenment, but we do believe without too much doubt that *characters* believe in it; as motivation, it works. (The only thing it might be compared to in this regard is money, but that's an essay for another day.) We do not question the assumption that people want to get closer to one another, that they will move heaven and earth in an attempt to achieve closeness, and that they will grieve mightily for the loss of that closeness. One cannot, as a writer, place patriotism at the center of a novel without shoring it up and explaining it quite a bit; ditto spiritual belief. But intimacy—whether it's romantic love, bonds with one's children or one's parents, intimacy among friends, even intimacy with objects; intimacy found or lost—is a sure thing, a state of affairs that can quickly undo a writer wishing to create art and not schlock.

I would counter Gornick's argument with the supposition that the dilemma the writer faces isn't that no one believes in love since 1968, but the opposite: the idea that intimacy is a self-evident good is so omnipresent that we don't even notice it. (I am indebted, here, to Elizabeth Povinelli's argument to this effect in her book *The Empire of Love,* which looks critically at what she terms "the intimacy diaspora" after the Enlightenment.) It's all too easy to throw a little intimacy, especially damaged intimacy, at a narrative to get it to seem serious and literary. Like corn syrup, it fills stuff out and makes it tasty. We're accustomed to its value. To which the struggling (always struggling) writer might well respond, So what? Intimacy *does* matter. What's the harm in relying on that? Don't we come to literature to try to understand what it is to be alive? Aren't we all trying to connect?

The harm, it seems to me as a struggling writer among other struggling writers, is that piety of any kind is never especially good for art. Characters can, and should, believe in all kinds of things, passionately and with brilliant wrongheadedness, but the book is, generally speaking, up to something else, something broader, something less sure of itself. Questions the writer might ask herself as she struggles to bring a sense of intimacy onto the page are, What assumptions am I making about what intimacy is? What received

ideas about intimacy am I perhaps unwittingly re-
producing? Many might immediately think of demo-
graphic categories—cultural assumptions that this sort
of person can't be with that sort of person; this one is
the wrong gender, race, age, body size for that one; intimacies such as domestic heterosexual love, preferably
with children, are the Big Stories and everything else
is a footnote or a curiosity. One might question these
assumptions.

One might also question easy gender stereotypes
about intimacy: women only want love and men only
want sex; women are better at intimacy than men; female friendship is always fraught with poisonous com-
petitiveness, especially for male attention; mothers
resent daughters; fathers abandon sons; women are
needy and manipulative; men are disappointing and
selfish; and so on. While one is at it, one could also
question received ideas about sex and sexual identity:
men are dogs and women are victims; sex within marriage is always boring and adultery is always thrilling
but emotionally false; women are dying to get married; gay men are promiscuous and amusing; lesbians
are hyperdomestic and faithful; bisexuals are untrust-
worthy tricksters who probably don't even really exist;
female orgasm is a difficult and often comic pursuit;
children being sexually abused feel numb; orgasm is always pleasurable; real sex is between people who are in

love and any other kind of sex is shallow and empty; one-night stands make you feel sad and sticky the next day; men with younger partners are lucky and women with younger partners are pathetic and probably have had bad plastic surgery; mothers don't have sex; fathers never get as much sex as they want and will inevitably turn to the (female, nubile, witless or sometimes conniving) babysitter; "foreplay" is a category; "slut" is a category; everyone's primary drive is sexual; sexual identity is fixed at the age of three. And so on. As one who teaches writing, I've read a supernatural amount of fiction that traffics in ideas and judgments about all kinds of intimacy that, at the very least, might be brought to the level of consciousness before being committed to the page.

But beyond these received ideas, cultural anxieties, and judgments, the writer might also ask herself if she is really so sure about what she's describing, if she has looked closely enough at the bond she is exploring in her work. Let us take, for instance, a well-worn cultural stereotype: the older, successful man with the younger, pretty woman on his arm. Often, one of two assumptions immediately spring onto the page. The first is that he is making use of her as sex toy and badge of his prowess (see: *The Dying Animal, Rabbit Redux,* etc.). The second is that she is making use of him as financial mark or psychological cat's paw (see: the film *The Blue*

Angel, Of Human Bondage, etc.). In the first scenario, he will inevitably trade her in for an even younger, newer model, particularly as his prowess declines. In the second scenario, she will ruin his life and perhaps, one way or another, he will end up dead, either literally or figuratively. If one proceeds from either of these two assumptions, the story writes itself. In the first scenario, he must be powerful, vain, and cold and she must be nothing but her physical beauty. In the second scenario, she must be a dark temptress and he must be repressed, tragic, possibly foolish, definitely balding. Humiliation must be part of the emotional tapestry; secondary characters must offer warnings that go unheeded; the power of illusion and self-delusion must be part of the theme. Comic set pieces can be expected.

Why bother even writing the rest or, indeed, reading it? We've already decided that we know what the intimacy between these two must be, we're sure of what they say to one another in the dark, we've assigned it a low value on the intimacy scale that forecloses on surprise, certainly on any real pleasure or dramatic tension in their union. All that's left to the writer is coloring in the outlines with more or less wit and with greater or lesser degrees of empathy. But what if the writer allows that she doesn't necessarily know what goes on between these two? What if she pauses to look closer? What if, for instance, the older man is an eminent artist in a wheelchair and the younger woman found herself, to her own surprise, falling passionately in love with him? What if the older man is white and the younger woman is African American? What if she is still deeply connected to the female lover she lived with for twelve years? What if the older man delights in the younger woman, but also envies her the freedom, on all levels, that is slipping from him every day? What if she's an aspiring artist, but not a very good one? What if he knows this but doesn't tell her, out of love? What if she knows that he knows this, too, but doesn't tell him, also out of love? What are her feelings as she wheels him up over a curb, the heavy wheelchair barking her shin? What are his? What do these two say to one another in the dark?

And so on. One doesn't have to ask if this older man and younger woman have produced the ideals of the Enlightenment in each other to be interested in what goes on between them or, possibly, to find meaning, resonance, and unexpected revelations in their story. Nor does one have to champion this pair and hand out narrative rewards in compensation for their cultural suffering—prejudice against the disabled, racism, homophobia. Maybe they live happily ever after, maybe they don't; maybe the intimacy between them has revelations to offer about love, or maybe it doesn't bear on love (or hate) at all. The Great Theme here at the end of the day could be art, it could be mortality and the power of time, it could be an inchoate dissonance between human beings that suggests the limits of intimacy, however strongly felt. It could also, as the conventions with which I began suggested, be a story of use. There's no reason to take that off the table as a possibility. However, it isn't the *only* possible story. In life, that isn't the case; why should it be the case in art?

It was Oscar Wilde who quipped, "Life imitates Art far more than Art imitates Life." Or, as Joan Didion put it in a kinder mode, "We tell ourselves stories in order to live." When we come to the page hoping to reveal something about intimacy, it is all too easy to force the rough, wayward, polyphonous, uncertain nature of this phenomenon into shapes that we already know and then come to foregone conclusions. We are anxious about intimacy, we crave it and fear it, and as a culture we can have a low tolerance for its essentially mercurial nature. One of the quiet implications of Nan Goldin's work, for instance, is the durational aspect of a photograph: it is the medium of the glimpse, the moment, the blink of an eye. Photographer and subject are linked in the image for a few seconds at best. Part of the pleasure of looking at her work is the viewer's subliminal knowledge of this; it is the shadow and subtext of the human connections Goldin has spent her career composing.

One word for low-level writing about intimacy might be *sentimental,* a term that can apply equally to romance novels, to stories of the deaths of children from cancer, and to narratives about middle-aged male professors having affairs with female students. In any or many of these, and in other examples of sentimentality, the writer's wishes and values override anything in the experience of the characters that doesn't fit the writer's fondest hopes: true love will prevail over every circumstance and result in marriage; the dying child will offer life wisdom to everyone around him; sex with the female student will be a mind-blowing, life-altering experience (for him). The emotions one might wish to have—enduring love, transcendence, lust—which are coincidentally the most socially acceptable emotions in each of their respective situations, are slathered thickly over the story, muffling the emotions that might be more complex, more resistant, more ambiguous. (J. M. Coetzee's *Disgrace* is one of the few novels that comes to mind in which sex between a male professor and a female student is presented in complex double focus— as an act of desperation and passion for him, and as a chillier, more coercive experience for her, yet one she chooses.) On the level of craft, this is a counterintuitive state of affairs—doesn't every writer wish to be original?—but every writer is also a reader, and readers want to be gratified, particularly when it comes to

matters of the heart. Intimacy is such an, as it were, intimate area that even as we long to look at it, we are
afraid to look too long or too closely. It can be too vulnerable to bear the idea that negative capability is as
constitutive of intimacy as it is of, say, artistic inspira-
tion. And in the former, one is much more often naked,
literally or figuratively or both.

Recently, I went to the studio of a photographer
friend who was working on a series of photos about
specialized forms of bondage. There, I watched a naked
woman encase herself in a balloon. It's one of the
lesser-known fetishes, but apparently one that inspires
unusual devotion. With the help of two others, the
woman inserted herself into the inflated balloon, which
was perhaps six feet high and three feet wide, and the
others taped off the opening, leaving the woman to
stand inside for a time. The inflated balloon was trans-
lucent, which meant that the woman, visually, had a
muzzy, dreamlike quality. Somehow, perhaps because
of the balloon's curves, she looked smaller than in real
life, like the hologram of Princess Leia in *Star Wars*
or Auntie Em inside the crystal ball in *The Wizard
of Oz*. She kept up a light, soft, steady tread with her
bare feet, which steadied the balloon in place without tearing it. Watching her, I was both fascinated and
uncomfortable in a way I couldn't articulate. When I
told the story afterward of watching the woman in the

balloon, the first reaction of many was that the balloon must be a womblike environment and this must be part of the impulse, to return to the safety of the womb. This is certainly one aspect, at least of what the scene looked like from the outside.

However, the idea that this scene was primarily fetal didn't touch on what else I saw, which was the extraordinary beauty of the woman once she was encased; the irreal quality; the claustrophobic glamour; the fragility of both balloon and woman; and the sense that we were looking at a gorgeous creature whom we could not touch and who could not touch any of the four of us who were in the studio that afternoon. Nor, of course, does the primal understanding of this scenario entirely account for what lurked in all of our minds: there is a limited amount of oxygen inside a balloon, and while it isn't necessarily fatally threatening to be there, suffocation is one of the notes that the image strikes, a possibility with which it toys. When I told the story to others, I told all of these parts, but I didn't tell the other part, the part that it took me weeks to understand. When I looked at the woman in the balloon, I felt a tremendous sadness and a certain amount of fear: Why, I wondered, did she feel compelled to do this difficult thing, create this extraordinary technology to get closer to something, some state, that she couldn't reach otherwise? It seemed so hard, to expose her to so much mockery and exploitation—look at the freak inside the balloon!—and to bespeak such intense loneliness. It was as if she was a Houdini of her own inner life, binding herself to get to herself in a way she couldn't do effortlessly, in daily life.

I didn't tell this part of the story, because it was so clearly my projection of her emotions—the emotions of a complete stranger—and potentially far too revealing about me. I don't think of myself this way, as a Houdini of my inner life, but why was that such a strong reaction of mine, and why did that idea frighten me so? Is it an image, perhaps, of writing, that terribly difficult technology we use to produce the sense of an inner life on the page? Some more personal nightmare? I still don't know. I was also reluctant to risk being seen as critical or uncool, shocked by such an innocent, pneumatic fetish. So I told the story as an adventure in modern lifestyles, more or less, and I included many fascinating physical details.

If I were writing this scene into a story, there are several potentially sentimental paths to take with it. The first is comic—clowns, the sound when the balloon popped (which it did, eventually), latex, Sally Rand, etc. The second is sexual—her being turned on inside the balloon, breasts and balloons, condoms and balloons, people masturbating outside the balloon, etc. The third is female psychosexual tragic—the lack of oxygen equals cultural gender oppression, she's a prisoner inside the balloon or inside her own desire to be imprisoned within the balloon, her mother is tying off the balloon opening, her father is tying off the balloon opening, etc.

All of these are plausible, of course, but none of them goes anywhere near the uneasy space between me and her that I still can't entirely express, and none of them allows her beauty to matter on any level other than the sheerly physical (slapstick, porn, enslavement). All three of these narratives are what we might expect to see and none of them allows for what I didn't expect to feel: fear and sorrow and enchantment, intermixed. All three, it might be noted, also expose the woman inside the balloon as a character who is reduced to type—clown, sex object, or victim—and none of them exposes me as the one who is choosing to tell her story. In this way, sentiment also functions protectively, as fig leaf and veil for the author. Her vulnerability touched on a vulnerability within me that I didn't understand, but any of these sentimental paths would blot that out and save me both the trouble of trying to articulate it and the potential arduousness of even attempting to do so. What was she doing in there? Why did I imagine what she was doing in there in the way that I did? Why am I still thinking about it? What did we, peering at her inside the balloon, look like to her?

I haven't written this scene into a story, except

insofar as this book might be considered a story, a story of stories. But if I were to write it into a story, I might begin with the possibility that the scene of the woman in the balloon may not be entirely knowable or fixed, that it might always bob away from the boundaries of whatever narrative it produces. A simpler way to say this would be that, naked though she was, the woman in the balloon retained an essential privacy. There may well be a vast space between the experience for her and the experience of each viewer. If I could, I would try to include that space.

The answer to the question Why meet?, I might suggest, is that we do not know in advance whom we will meet in art, what characters' meetings with one another will produce in them or in the world, nor do we know in advance what effect these crossings will have on us. We sometimes know what we wish, what we dread, what we expect. But we do not know what will happen if only we have the courage to look closely. Intimacy is not a good place to go for ideals, humans being what they are. But it is a tremendously fertile zone for all the emotions and mental states for which we have a name, and many for which we have no name at all.

Meeting in the White Space

One of the most complex and mobile intimacies produced on the page is that between reader and writer. As writers, we engage this space between with every letter we put down, every comma, every sentence, paragraph, and scene. It's a curious business, writing toward a reader whom we can't see, don't know, and who must be multiple, or at least we hope so. We write toward a point that cannot be fixed in number, space, or time. This point is, on the one hand, an ever-changing crowd, and, on the other hand, an abyss. Questions such as Who is your ideal reader? and Who is your audience? obscure the larger, more unsettling truth, which is that the writer is continually engaging an unknowable Other, a protean ghost. In a conventional, realistic piece of fiction, this protean Other, this reader, is treated as if he or she isn't there and isn't needed. The world of the book is a bustling, self-contained whole; the fourth wall is unbroken. The reader is asked to peer in, to witness, to identify, to like and dislike, to be moved, and so on, but the essential privacy of the separate spheres of book and reader, like the essential privacy of the woman in the balloon, is respected. It's an illusion, of course, but it allows the reader to relax into the dreamspace of the fiction unself-consciously.

In other works of fiction, the space between reader and writer is more kinetic, more acknowledged, less reliable, and the interdependence between the two is more exposed. The reader is not allowed to relax into the dreamspace of the book or story but is, instead, continually jolted awake, as it were. A modern classic of this genre is Italo Calvino's *If on a winter's night a traveler*, which begins, "You are about to begin reading Italo Calvino's new novel, *If on a winter's night a traveler*. Relax. Concentrate. Dispel every other thought. Let the world around you fade." This is very funny, because, obviously: fat chance of relaxing now that he's made you so hyperaware that you're reading. Calvino seems to be an eye looking out from the page at your eye, or your I, pun intended, and just to be even more contrary, he insists on being as hard to pin down as "you," his invisible cocreator. He writes, "You prepare to recognize the unmistakable tone of the author. . . . But now that you think about it, who ever said this author had an unmistakable tone? On the contrary, he is known as an author who changes greatly from one book to the next. And in these very changes you recognize him as himself."

In subsequent "chapters," a different novel begins every time, and in each of these novels the reader is invoked as the one reading the novel, the one without whom the novel cannot exist ("You have now read about thirty pages." "You have entered the novel." "The plane is landing; you have not managed to finish the novel"). Frequently, the metaphysics of reading itself is discussed. The materiality of the page, and the elusiveness and permeability of the text, are continually subjects as well. "The book," Calvino writes, "should be the written counterpart of the unwritten world; its subject should be what does not exist and cannot exist except when written, but whose absence is obscurely felt by that which exists, in its own incompleteness." "That which exists, in its own incompleteness," being you, reader. The topos, the meeting ground, for fiction that makes powerful use of the relationship between reader and writer is white space, which we can simultaneously consider to be white space on the page and the blankness, the open air, between reader and writer.

In *If on a winter's night a traveler* there is a playfulness and lightness in Calvino's dance with the reader that charms, even riddles, but doesn't truly intrude or challenge. The "incompleteness" to which he alludes is not a hole in the self as much as it as a place where the threads fray, where the raggedy seams of being are visible. Within one book, one self, many may reside with equal probability. The white space between chapters in *If on a winter's night a traveler* is akin to the subjunctive space in the Maxwell and Bowen novels I discussed earlier: the *if* is a fold, another tale, a space of nearly limitless possibility, a perpetual opportunity for seduction. "I put my eye to the spyglass and train it on the reader," Calvino writes. "Between her eyes and the page a white butterfly flutters. . . . The unwritten world has its climax in that butterfly. The result at which I must aim is something specific, intimate, light."

In other works of fiction, that white space between reader and writer is not a white butterfly. It is more treacherous ground, the whiteness of ice that might crack or has cracked, and readers may find that their participation involves risks that are not as metaphysical or lepidopteristic. In two contemporary works of fiction, Joan Didion's *Play It As It Lays* and Percival Everett's *The Water Cure,* the space between reader and writer is roiled, uncertain, and the questions it asks the reader are more often ethical or moral than they are cerebral. Both are confessions, in a way, but of what crimes, and to what ends are not immediately apparent. It's clear, however, that the reader will not be allowed a cozy seat in the anonymity of the confession booth as confessor. Instead, the reader is continually dropped into various uneasy roles as voyeur, enabler, terrorist, and confidant to secrets that are very uncomfortable to know.

Maria Wyeth, the complicated heroine of *Play It As*

It Lays, is made primarily out of white space, out of ellipses, rumor, innuendo, gossip, banal phone conversations, images from B movies, absence, every cliché about Hollywood ever invented, intersecting highways, invisibility, and a kind of fretful, compulsive need to stay in motion without actually getting anywhere. *Play It As It Lays,* published in 1970, is a confession, essentially. Maria, thirty-one, is telling her story from a cushy mental institution, where she's gone, or been sent, after committing a terrible crime, or what we're told is a terrible crime. Up until this point, Maria has been a B-movie actress in Hollywood, married to a director named Carter. The high point of her career thus far was playing a girl raped by a motorcycle gang in a movie called *Angel Beach;* otherwise, she mostly ornaments Los Angeles, looking good in a silver vinyl dress, driving too fast, taking drugs, and going to parties. She has a small daughter with an unspecified, debilitating medical condition who is institutionalized, and this is the one part of her life about which Maria is unabashedly tender; otherwise, she seems to be glamorously alienated and empty. Her marriage to Carter is coming apart, and her career is going nowhere.

The literal action of the book is Maria's breakdown—the slow breakup with Carter, some cruddy sex, an illegal abortion, and then the climactic scene in a motel near a movie set in the desert, her "crime," what the other characters refer to as her "murder" of another character, named BZ. What actually happens in this scene is that BZ, an insanely jaded gay Hollywood insider straight out of the pages of Jacqueline Susann, kills himself by taking a handful of pills, and Maria, who is lying next to him at the time, does nothing to stop him. This is her crime, her sin, and the book, like all confessions, is itself the mark of Maria's hope even in the midst of an overwhelming sense of pointlessness, existential dread, and anomie.

The opening lines of the book are, "What makes Iago evil? some people ask. I never have to ask." What follows, however, is actually an argument for how it is that we choose to live anyway, even in the face of our knowledge that evil is inevitable, pervasive, and natural. BZ, who is in many ways Maria's doppelgänger, her secret sharer, the one who recognizes her and whom she recognizes, kills himself while Maria, who has just as much reason to do so, doesn't. It's that choice, that flip of the coin, that the book attempts to understand. The novel closes with these lines:

> I know what "nothing" means, and keep on playing.
>> Why, BZ would say.
>> Why not, I say.

The book, and Maria, are constructed of tiny "chapters" that are like the few words you might barely be able to scratch out on the rim of the abyss. Here is chapter 52 in its entirety:

> Maria made a list of things she would never do. She would never: *walk through the Sands or Caesar's alone after midnight.* She would never: *ball at a party, do S-M unless she wanted to, borrow furs from Abe Lipsey, deal.* She would never: *carry a Yorkshire in Beverly Hills.*

And this is chapter 8:

> "You haven't asked me how it went after we left Anita's," BZ said.
>
> "How did it go," Maria said without interest.
>
> "Everybody got what he came for."
>
> "Don't you ever get tired of doing favors for people?"
>
> There was a long silence. "You don't know how tired," BZ said.

Didion makes Maria out of these fragmentary scenes, and she also switches between a first-person narration from Maria's point of view and a third-person narration. These do not alternate in a predictable pattern. Roughly—very roughly—the first-person narration opens and closes the book and the third-person narration occupies most of the middle of the book, as if Maria were making a movie of her own life and running it in her head at the institution. But sometimes the first-person narration just drops in unpredictably and then just as unpredictably departs. The organizing principle, in other words, is intuitive and uneven, and its unevenness constitutes a fault line, a crack, that runs through the character, the novel, and, by implication, the human condition. Maria is composed of a collage of gazes, in a way—in addition to the first-person and the close third-person, there are sections in which she is described by other characters, mostly unflatteringly; and there are also several celluloid Marias—the Maria who's the chick in *Angel Beach*, and a cinema verité Maria shot by Carter early in their marriage.

This uneven, contradictory, sometimes self-canceling, oddlot jumble, these concentrated shots floating in white space, do not give us Maria "whole" or in some final form. They give us Maria shattered, scattered, and spiraling— she moves around herself, probing, both in control and not in control of her own narrative. She is composed of her own self-consciousness, but she is also—like any actress, and, indeed, any person—explicitly composed of the highly partial and manipulative gazes of others.

We are explicitly included among these others. By compiling this scrapbook of gazes and opinions, Didion invites us to contemplate our own judgments, decisions, perspective, and possibly uncertain answers to the questions that not only face Maria, but also compose Maria. As befits a novel about a movie actress, we are an audience, but unlike the audience in a movie theater, we are not permitted the anonymity and boundaryless-ness of the dark. We are not, as in *Scopophilia,* invited into the limerence of voyeuristic identification. Instead, we are caught looking in the glare of the white space, caught peering and probing, dissecting, or, possibly worse, caught in the act of trying to glue together that which is hopelessly broken.

In chapter 52, for instance, the list of things that Maria would "never do" is a list of her rapidly dimin-ishing options as her marriage and her career disinte-grate. The reader must know that the list is a lie, that, in fact, Maria is making a list of what she is most likely about to do, or has done already. The reader must also know, must notice, how limited a list it is. Nowhere on it, for instance, is *go back to school* or *get out of Hollywood.* Without this knowledge of what kind of woman Maria is and what she's becoming, the chapter makes no sense; Didion does not allow the reader to play innocent. The next stop for Maria in this world is some form of prostitution to a greater or lesser degree of tawdriness. The Yorkie, here, would be the high end of that spectrum. In the white space around chapter 52, the place where the reader meets the text, is world-liness, the assumption of a shared sensibility that would never bother to ask what makes Iago evil. Bail on that complicity, and you bail on the novel itself. You literally cannot read it. The emptiness around the text is the emptiness of a dead-end street at night, the few words like the click of heels on the pavement. If you don't shudder, you are either terribly naive or stone-cold insensitive.

Even more problematic for the reader is the complicity with Maria's radical passivity, a passivity that results in the death of BZ. In the penultimate scene of the book, BZ turns up at the motel where Maria is staying. He has a bottle of Seconal and the clear intention to commit suicide with the pills. Maria doesn't stop him. Instead, she holds his hand and falls asleep as he kills himself. Again, a certain kind of knowingness is invoked. BZ says to Maria, "You and I, we *know* something. . . . We've been out there where nothing is." And, a few lines later, when she tells him not to take the pills, he says, "Don't start faking me now." She doesn't. At this point, it's a bit late in the game for readers to start faking, either, to pretend that they don't know about all that nothing around and within Maria, and by implication around BZ. It's too late to retreat into a generic optimism about the value of human life. The existential trap has been sprung. Each of the fragments up to this point has depended on the reader's knowledge and understanding of what isn't being said, being shown, the reader's silent nod. We know why the list in chapter 52 is so short. If one allows that there can be a pain in being alive that nothing can assuage, and if one believes, further, that all human beings have a right to their own destiny, then it must follow that BZ has a right to his own death and Maria's sleep is just.

This, however, is not a comfortable conclusion to reach. It seems inhuman. If the expanse in Calvino's novel of novels was infinite and endlessly revisable, here, that same expanse equalizes suicide as a plausible choice. Freedom also means the freedom to choose one's death. It must, or the concept has no weight at all. The openness and exposed interdependence with the reader that was a dance in Calvino's book is, here, the raised eyebrow, the piercing look that says *Don't pretend you don't know.* Didion dares the reader to look away, to blink. She will not make it easy. She does not ask the reader to be sympathetic to Maria, to see that she's had it tough, that she's more or less alone in the world, that she's doing her best. She's not doing her best. In fact, she's not doing much at all. Instead, she's floating, she's drifting, she's falling. What Didion asks of us is not sympathy but a degree of participation in Maria's self-construction, and self-destruction, that binds us into a profound intimacy with her. We helped invent her, and we know that. We can't say that all we did was buy a ticket to the show. Our fingerprints are all over the novel. The white space, the space between in *Play It As It Lays,* is like the blank piece of paper that the cops give the perp in myriad television shows and movies, saying, *Start writing. Tell us in your own words what happened.* The piece of paper is being given to us.

Percival Everett's *The Water Cure* frames itself, as it were, as a confession as well, and here the crime is quite blatant. "I am guilty," writes the main character, Ishmael Kidder. "I executed these actions with not only deliberation and premeditation but with zeal and paroxysm and purpose. . . . The true answer to your question is shorter than the lie. Did you? I did." What Kidder did was find, capture, and torture a man who might have been—but probably is not—the man who raped and murdered his eleven-year-old daughter. Kidder is crazed by grief; who wouldn't be? He explains, "With my vengeance eyes burning the horizon for Man X, will Man Y do, and will he satisfy my desire, and am I correct not only in my identification of Man Y as Man X, but also in my belief that there is a Man X at all?" This is the loopy, darkly poignant logic of a man struggling with unbearable emotions. The novel, published in 2007, makes explicit references to waterboarding, Guantánamo, and Abu Ghraib, clearly making a comparison between the use of torture as an interrogation method following the attacks of September 11, 2001, and the use of torture as revenge. In the same way that the United States deployed the lie that Iraq was responsible for the attacks of September 11 to go to war with that country, Kidder (pun intended, we may be sure) is using a lie, or an illusion, to satisfy his rage. Ethical and political questions are openly in play; the global tragedy is mapped onto the novel's domestic tragedy.

The book begins with an image of a mark on a page under which are the words ". . . so we induce"; the next page is blank save for the word *and;* the page after is also blank save for the word *find;* the text proper begins with the words "the arduous nowhere." The novel proceeds as a series of fragments of various sizes separated by white space; the fragments are composed of the narrative of the murder and subsequent torture of the maybe-murderer, reflections on the nature of language, jokes, riddles, drawings that seem to have been made by a child, bits from Aristotle and other philosophers, reflections on skydiving and welding and geometry, lines written in French and what seems to be a faux Middle English, among other topics and modes. Ishmael is a romance novelist, under another name, so the novel also includes passages from his pseudonymous work and meditations on his conflicted attitude toward it. The fragments encourage us to think with Ishmael, to take leaps across the white space of connections among categories—What does welding have to do with Aristotle? What does a failed marriage have to do with geometry? Ishmael, we are told quite late in the book, is African American and the murderer is white, but where do we put race in this story, this series of discontinuous fragments? What is "the arduous nowhere"?

If Maria was composed of a variety of sometimes contradictory gazes and opinions and versions of herself authored by others, Ishmael is composed of a variety of sometimes contradictory thoughts, observations, conundrums, emotional positions, and languages of his own making. *The Water Cure* is a story about torture, but it is also a monologue delivered by a man, a writer, who doesn't entirely make sense to himself, who invites the reader to consider the fragments he has shored against his ruin without ever offering us the option of reshaping those fragments into a glibly heroic narrative. If the novel were a collage that the reader could, potentially, rearrange at will, there is no arrangement that would produce Ishmael as a noble, righteous avenger of wrongdoing or a suffering victim. Like Maria, Ishmael considers himself to be many things, but innocent is never one of them. He wouldn't ask what makes Iago evil, either. Having, like Maria, established his guilt in the opening pages of the book, he also denies the reader the shelter of an ignorant innocence. Didion refused us this innocence by making the book unreadable to the naive. Ishmael binds the reader into complicity via a sympathetic response few could refuse to feel: that is, via our outrage and sadness at this horrible murder of a child, the child of our main character, our narrator, our point of identification.

At first, we don't put up much resistance to this complicity. Identifying with Ishmael's hatred is only natural; one might question one's own humanity if one didn't share his ire. Whose anger wouldn't be extreme? As Ishmael stalks the murderer of his child, he tells us, "I was the cop and the judge and the jury and the executioner and god, and god, was I filled with hatred, sweet righteous hatred." Not long after this moment, the man who might or might not be the murderer is in the trunk of Ishmael's car; Ishmael has slammed the other man on the back of the head with a bat and bound and gagged him with duct tape. Chillingly, Ishmael doesn't kill him right away: "I needed him alive so that I could have his life, possess his life, take his life, needed to have him see his life stolen." Now, queasily, we begin to see that Ishmael isn't taking revenge on the murderer of his daughter in payment for her life; instead, he is exacting a slow, painful, possibly endless revenge on a stranger for someone—probably not this man in the trunk at all—having destroyed *Ishmael's* life and sentenced him to an existence that will never be free of sorrow, guilt, and rage. Like John Wayne's pathological character obsessed with finding the pioneer girl captured by Native Americans in the John Ford film *The Searchers,* Ishmael's drive for vengeance has, somewhere along the line, become a quest to redress an injury done not to the victimized girl, but to him, to his sense of self.

At this point, the reader might become very uneasy, but it's too late, because the stranger is already in the trunk of the car. Indeed, it's too late to back out of the book at all, because the scenes of what Ishmael actually did to the stranger don't occur until midway through the narrative. We have already seen the unbearable grief of the parents, the battered and invaded body of the child, the childish drawings. We have already agreed that we would kill a man who would do a thing like that, that such a man deserves to die. Who cares if he dies fast or slowly? We have already thought with Ishmael about the unexpected conjunctions of language, deep feeling, and philosophy. But as the wronged person being avenged subtly shifts from daughter to father, and as the details of the capture and torture emerge, and as the fact that this is probably not the murderer at all gets louder, like Poe's telltale heart, we find ourselves holding a bloody bag that we might not be entirely sure we want. How, we might wonder, did we quite get here?

> His skin is pink, his nails yellowed and hard and
> grooved crosswise, his knuckles hairy, some of them,
> his skin pink and cracked, dry, chapped patterns

formed in the creases between his thumbs and fore-
fingers, as if ready to split, bleed, or fold open from
itself to reveal the pink meat within, and as I stretch
the silver duct tape taut then lay it against that skin,
the skin of his knobbed wrists, crossed one over the
other, I can see the yellow hairs seeming to rise to
meet the adhesive, the ripping sound of the tape peel-
ing from itself filling the room, then ceasing, leaving
the silence clean enough to find the small sounds of
this finite world, the sound of my own heart, surpris-
ingly slow and steady, the sound of my breathing, a
slight rattle in my chest, and of his breathing, clearer
than my own, but rapid and short and small, and
then the sound of one of his nervous yellowed nails
scratching at the fir plank against which he is tied, the
blond wood giving up a worm of a sliver that crawls
under his nail into his flesh, and I imagine that the
pain is reconnecting him with the world, and so I yank
off another length of tape and let the noise hang in
the air so that I can again have his senses.

Too late, we understand that Ishmael wants to possess and control the other man at the root in the same
way that this crime against his daughter has possessed
and controlled him. Ishmael doesn't want to commit
murder; he wants to commit soul murder. In an in-
version of the famous lightbulb-filled basement room

of the oppressed African American narrator in Ralph Ellison's *Invisible Man,* Ishmael fills his basement torture chamber with mirrors. He says to his victim, "I want you to see all these other people and wonder which one of you is feeling the pain, which of you is feeling the pain more, less, which of you is only watching and feeling nothing." And, later, "I want you to pray to me, pray that I don't come back and that I never leave you." What Ishmael wants, in other words, is a profound, lifetime, terror-filled intimacy with this man, this stranger, in retribution for the horrible act of violence against Ishmael's daughter. Ishmael's revenge will be a closeness in which the other man can no longer experience himself and can only experience Ishmael, delivered as pure fear. He wants the other man, as in the passage quoted, to be breath to breath with him, forever, and never to know again whose breath is whose.

This is merciless. It is, indeed, a crime, a crime far worse than killing the actual murderer would have been. And can we, as readers, distinguish ourselves from Ishmael? Can we say with any degree of certainty that Ishmael's unbearable loss wouldn't motivate us to wish to inflict that same degree of loss on someone, anyone? The irresistible sentiment that we grasped unthinkingly at the beginning of the novel turns out to be filled with nettles that can't be picked out easily. The distance from the childish drawing to the duct tape might be less than we thought. Everett deploys intimacy—the intimacy between parent and child, between writer and reader, between tortured and torturer—to ask profoundly uncomfortable ethical, emotional, political, and moral questions. The space between, here, is less than a shared breath, an ellipsis, a break in the text, a hall of mirrors, in which love and terror, writer and reader, are indistinguishable. We have seen that meeting in the dark can be fatal; now we see that meeting in the white space, in the blankness, may be just as perilous, if not more so.

Distance

In section two of the ten-part Yoko Tawada story "The Bath," a photographer named Xander attempts to take a picture of the narrator, a Japanese woman. The shoot doesn't go well. The camera makes the woman anxious ("the lens was trying to trap me"), and the man can't seem to get the image he seeks. "Can't you look a little more Japanese?" he says. "This is for a travel poster." The woman remains uneasy about the camera, thinking, "If it wanted to learn my soul's secrets, I had nothing to worry about, since there weren't any. But this camera was trying to capture my skin." When Xander develops the photographs, the woman is invisible in them, a condition that, he tells her, happened "because you don't have a strong enough sense of yourself as Japanese." In order to address this problem, Xander covers the woman's face with thick powder, lines her eyes, paints her lips the color of her lips, and blackens her already black hair. He marks her face with an *x*, his mark, and snaps the picture. The *x*, reports the woman, "stopped the light from playing and crucified the image of a Japanese woman onto the paper."

This is a parable about race, and perhaps about gender, but it also touches on the conundrum of how to see, and how difficult it is to see directly. We have

considered thus far the various uses of the space between in rendering intimacy in fiction—a few of those
charged spaces being the subjunctive, the world, the
image, the dark, and white space—but we have yet to
consider why it is, or how it is, that a space between
is necessary at all. Why must this topos be created in
order for the reader to apprehend intimacy? Why can't
we simply experience it directly, as we do in life? Why
must we, as it were, climb inside a balloon to feel the
most primal, the most powerful human emotion—i.e.,
connectedness? To borrow the clichés of a million pop
songs, what's so hard about just saying "I love you"?

And yet, rendered that way—*I love you*—the phrase
has no weight; ditto *I hate you, he loves her, she loves
her, they all loved one another once, he despised him,*
and so on. We don't feel these phrases as meaningful,
nor would we be likely to if they were attached to names
of characters. In order to feel the weight, paradoxically,
we sometimes have to use a mirror, a distorted image
that will make the "true" image appear. We grow closer
through distance, through a gap of time or space or
context across which we are somehow better able to
apprehend connection than if that which we seek were
directly at hand.

A particularly potent example of the necessity of distance in fully apprehending intimacy is Toni Morrison's

Beloved. Set in Ohio in 1873, it is the story of Sethe, a former slave, who did a terrible thing when she was still enslaved at a plantation called Sweet Home: she killed her two-year-old daughter by slashing her throat rather than see the child go on to live a life of slavery. Eighteen years later, that daughter, who was never named except for the single word on her tombstone, *Beloved,* returns in altered form as a strange young woman and takes up residence with Sethe and her family. What follows is simultaneously reunion and exorcism as Sethe wrestles with her own past and her fractured psyche.

Much of Sethe's nearly impossible task has to do with unsayability, of which there are several layers at play in *Beloved.* The first, of course, is the institution of slavery itself, an atrocity of such magnitude that it can only, in a way, be seen in Sethe's terrible act. In other words, we can barely look at it directly; we can only truly, viscerally comprehend its horror in the horrible thing it causes Sethe to do. There are gruesome scenes of life under slavery in the novel, but they pale in comparison to Sethe killing her own small child. Death, her action suggests, is better than that life. We *see* the facts of slavery in the literal flashbacks to life at Sweet Home, but we *feel* the atrocity of slavery, we feel its weight, in the unspeakable murder of the child. The second unsayable thing is that very action; to kill one's own child is unthinkable, unbearable. But there's a third, subtler, equally disturbing layer of unsayability here, and this layer is where Morrison actually begins her extraordinary book.

As terrible as it is to kill one's own child, how much more terrible is it when that child returns from the grave, carrying an unimaginably heavy freight of guilt, terror, rage, need, and love? This, in its way, is even more unsayable—that as missed, as mourned, as that child is, to have that child *come back* after being murdered by her own mother is unbearable. One does not wish to say that, it's an unsayable thought, particularly addressed to a two-year-old girl: *stay dead.* But that ambivalence is exactly where Morrison pitches the tent of the novel. The book begins not during the plantation years, not in the time leading up to the terrible crime, but in the relatively peaceful aftermath—postslavery, postinfanticide. The book begins with something that is not only unsayable, but impossible: the child comes back to haunt her own mother. And, in fact, the first two sentences of the book are somewhat shocking: "124 was spiteful. Full of a baby's venom." (124 is the number of the house where Sethe and her surviving family live.)

A baby's *venom.* What a phrase. What a word choice. Not *anger,* not *rage,* not *tantrum,* not *sadness:* venom. Like a poisonous snake. *Spite.* And what this opening page goes on to describe is this ghost, this venomous baby, terrorizing Sethe and her other children so severely that Sethe's two sons just run away, leaving Sethe and her other daughter, Denver, at its mercy. "As soon as two tiny hand prints appeared in the cake," writes Morrison, the sons flee. That image of the little handprints in the cake—so domestic, so dear, so, even, sentimental—becomes an image of ominousness, terror, and mortal threat.

From here, Morrison ups the ante even further. When Beloved really reappears to begin her haunting in earnest, it is not in the form of handprints in a cake or as a two-year-old in a nightgown wafting transparently around the house at night. Beloved, as if she has grown older in real time along with everyone else, walks out of a stream one day as "a fully dressed woman." Sethe takes her in, not exactly able to understand at first why she's so drawn to this peculiar young woman. Beloved is thirsty, she has a telltale scar on her neck, and her skin is oddly new and soft. And though her physical form is that of a woman, emotionally she is still two years old. She is passionately attached to Sethe, guileless, sexually curious and omnivorous, constantly hungry, demanding, dear, and prone to terrible jealousy. She is an unhoused, infantile id, but with all the power and size of a full-grown adult.

Though the events in the past that are being mourned are dramatic indeed, the actual dramatic action of the book's present time is subtle, wayward, and difficult to describe. It's something closer to a love triangle, or several love triangles, as Beloved proceeds basically to seduce everyone in 124, than it is to, say, a murder mystery or even a ghost story. In overt terms, not much happens in *Beloved.* Sethe, Beloved, Denver, and Sethe's boyfriend, Paul D, all live in 124 in increasingly strained and emotionally extreme circumstances until Sethe stops being haunted by Beloved.

To stop being haunted by Beloved, Sethe has to do two things: she has to remember who Beloved is, that this is the child she killed; and, even more important, she has to fall in love with her utterly, completely, and unconditionally, in the way that a mother loves her child. Once she does these two things, she can be free. The book reaches its climax when Sethe does this, when she finally claims, "Beloved, she my daughter. She mine." And for about twenty pages after this point, the text of the book literally breaks down and fragments into prose poetry as Sethe, Beloved, and Denver declare their deep and abiding love for one another, without reservation. They all repeat some variation of "Beloved is mine," like a refrain. After this point, Beloved finally departs and 124 is no longer troubled.

What I think this suggests is that Morrison is addressing yet another layer of unsayability in *Beloved,* perhaps the deepest atrocity and wound of slavery, which is that, for the slave, it makes *love* an unsayable, a forbidden, word. If your children are literally going to be taken from you and sold, if you would rather kill them than see them live the life you've led, if human ties are continually broken, severed, and destroyed, then loving without reservation is a very, very dangerous thing to do. Love—ordinary, daily, open intimacy—becomes unsayable as a matter of survival. The novel, like the history of slavery, is filled with stories of lovers pulled apart, mothers giving up their children, fathers never even knowing they have any children, and people being used in monstrous ways that violate every human sense of trust and connection.

When Sethe makes her first, unsuccessful run toward freedom, she says, of getting away from Sweet Home, in Kentucky, with her children, "Look like I loved em more after I got here. Or maybe I couldn't love em proper in Kentucky because they wasn't mine to love. But when I got here [i.e., to freedom in Ohio], when I jumped down off that wagon—there wasn't nobody in the world that I couldn't love if I wanted to." It's significant that it is *after* this moment, this moment of unabashed love, that Sethe slashes Beloved's throat. The slavecatchers come to get them and she can't bear to take her children back to that life. She loves without reservation for the first time in her life, then has to kill what she loves, then is bound by melancholy until Beloved comes back and Sethe can finally say, again, that she loves her.

In the fractured world of *Beloved*, this is the most forbidden, the most unsayable emotion: this mother love, one of the most basic emotions we experience. It's worth noting in this regard that in Morrison's *Playing in the Dark: Whiteness and the Literary Imagination*, one of her most stinging critiques of Willa Cather's *Sapphira and the Slave Girl* revolves around Cather's racist idea in that novel that slave women don't care about their children, that they are "natally dead," that they will be complicit in the exploitation of their children. And I think that aspect of racism, its destruction of the ability to speak one's love freely, is why Morrison wrote the word *love*, bracketed by a few other letters, across the front of her book.

But would we have understood the weight of that word if we had not been brought to the brink of *almost not being able* to say, to feel, this essential emotion? Could we apprehend it without a mirror, in this case the mirror of another time, another place, a set of circumstances that nearly extinguish one of the most fundamental aspects of being human? Could we, in other words, feel the weight of that word weighed simply as itself? *Beloved* teaches us that it may be the case that, paradoxically, we feel the weight of that word more directly by experiencing the weight of the forces ranged against it, that we measure its power in the power of its cost. Over great distance, and through nearly unbearable loss, finally, we get closer.

Still Trying to See

Only connect. Wisely, Forster didn't specify who or how many would be connecting, nor what the nature of that connection might be. Intimacy in fiction can be rendered as a space between that is as close as a breath, or as great as a century. We hunger for intimacy in art, and yet what we hunger for is not always the happily ever after, the joyous reunion. I find, scribbled among the notes I made in the dark while I was watching the slide show in *Scopophilia,* "Making visible what, without you, I would perhaps have never seen." What Goldin might have been quoting, if anything, and to what image this phrase was attached, I neglected to write down. I left the specifics somewhere in the dark. But when I come to fiction, both as a reader and as a writer, I wish for it to make visible something that, without it, I would perhaps have never seen. The reason that I might not have seen it isn't that it is so rare, but that it can sometimes be nearly impossible to truly see that which is as omnipresent as air. The distance of art allows me to see the emotional medium that surrounds us all.

And so I am grateful for the company of these others that makes visible the invisible: among them, two children meeting in a strange house that is home to neither of them; a husband and wife who retain an obdurate foreignness to one another; a family at a dinner table; an odd pair of lovers; two women who know one another's secret; two men at sea; a torturer and his victim; mother and child; writer and reader. The space between any and all of these people is not easy to find or express. The tools used by the various writers to delineate them are inventive: the subjunctive, shared perspective, image, off-the-page implication, the deployment of white space, and so on.

One might conclude from this that unlikely intimacies require original narrative techniques, but it seems more likely to me that the space between is, itself, a terrain that requires inventiveness, daring, and perhaps a few unsettling ideas: that empathy for the other is not a luxury but a moral requirement, even of children; that deep love, even within a marriage, is not necessarily a reassuring or self-affirming experience; that intimacy can be communal, disembodied, and semiconscious; that the recognition, found through sex, that passes between any couple is rare, fragile, and can't be possessed; that the intimacy that seeks to destroy can be nearly indistinguishable from the sense of self. Perhaps the most fundamental idea that these writers share is the idea that every space between is unique and consequential; that it has its own duration, which is not necessarily equal to its importance; and that it requires a participation by its characters that is not predictable or automatic. Being a child, being in love, being in grief, being in a family, being undone, being in bed with someone else: we might think we know what these things mean, but, as these writers show us so well, we don't. We don't know anything about it.

Works Discussed

Baxter, Charles. *The Soul Thief.*

Bowen, Elizabeth. *The House in Paris.*

Calvino, Italo. *If on a winter's night a traveler,* trans. William Weaver.

Conrad, Joseph. *The Secret Sharer.*

Cooper, Dennis. *My Mark.*

Didion, Joan. *Play It As It Lays.*

Everett, Percival. *The Water Cure.*

Goldin, Nan. *Scopophilia.*

Gornick, Vivian. *The End of the Novel of Love.*

Larsen, Nella. *Passing.*

Lawrence, D. H. *The Rainbow.*

Maxwell, William. *So Long, See You Tomorrow.*

Morrison, Toni. *Beloved.*

Morrison, Toni. *Playing in the Dark: Whiteness and the Literary Imagination.*

Povinelli, Elizabeth. *The Empire of Love.*

Tawada, Yoko. "The Bath," in *Where Europe Begins,* trans. Susan Bernofsky.

Woolf, Virginia. *To the Lighthouse.*

STACEY D'ERASMO is the author of *The Sky Below*, a *New York Times* Notable Book of the Year and a *Los Angeles Times* Favorite Book of the Year; *A Seahorse Year;* and *Tea*, a *New York Times* Notable Book of the Year. A former Stegner Fellow and the recipient of a Guggenheim Fellowship in Fiction, she is an assistant professor at Columbia University. Her nonfiction work has appeared in the *New York Times Book Review*, the *New York Times Magazine, Bookforum, Boston Review, New England Review*, and *Ploughshares*, among other publications. Her fourth novel, *Wonderland*, will be published in 2014.

The text of *The Art of Intimacy: The Space Between* is set in Warnock Pro, a typeface designed by Robert Slimbach for Adobe Systems in 2000. Book design by Wendy Holdman. Composition by BookMobile Design & Digital Publisher Services, Minneapolis, Minnesota. Manufactured by Versa Press on acid-free 30 percent postconsumer wastepaper.